RAIL 150

The Stockton & Darlington Railway
and what followed

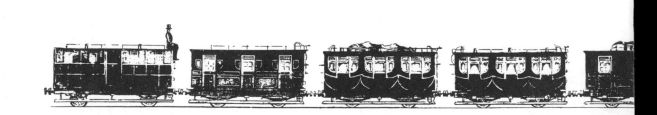

RAIL 150

The Stockton & Darlington Railway
and what followed

by Ken Hoole, Jack Simmons,
Michael Bonavia and Ian Waller
Edited by Jack Simmons

Eyre Methuen · London

First published 1975
by Eyre Methuen Ltd
11 New Fetter Lane, London EC4P 4EE
© 1975 The British Railways Board
Printed Offset Litho in Great Britain by
Cox & Wyman Ltd
Fakenham, Norfolk

ISBN 0 413 32300 5 (hardback)
ISBN 0 413 32310 2 (Methuen Paperback)

CONTENTS

ILLUSTRATIONS

FIGURES IN TEXT

MAPS

ACKNOWLEDGMENTS FOR ILLUSTRATIONS

The editor and the publishers are indebted to British Rail for permission to reproduce most of the pictures in this book; and, personally, to Mr W. Macdonald for his unwearied assistance in finding them. They are similarly obliged, in addition, to the following: Glasgow Museums (Plate II), Mr John Goss (Plates III, IV), Mr K. Hoole (Plates 1–3, 6–9, Fig. 2), Aberdeen University Library, G. W. Wilson Collection (Plates 12, 18, 29), London Transport (Plates 15, 28, 46, 73), The Science Museum (Fig. 1). The print from which Fig. 5 has been reproduced was kindly lent by Frank T. Sabin Ltd.

INTRODUCTION

This book appears as part of a celebration to commemorate the 150th anniversary of the opening of the Stockton & Darlington Railway, on 27 September 1825. It is important at the outset to make quite clear what that event really means.

The Stockton & Darlington was not the first railway. Railways had been working in different parts of England at least since the seventeenth century. It was not even the first public railway: that honour belongs to the Surrey Iron Railway, which was established under an Act of Parliament of 1801. The locomotives it used were not the first, either. George Stephenson had been building them for colliery lines since 1814, and he did not invent them. If they are to be ascribed to one inventor, it is undoubtedly Trevithick. Nor, finally, was the Stockton & Darlington the first railway to convey passengers. They had been carried in Wales from Swansea to Oystermouth since 1807, and in Scotland since 1817, between Kilmarnock and Troon.

But if the Stockton & Darlington was not the pioneer in any one of these important elements in what we think of now as a railway, it fused them together, to make an organism of a kind that had not been seen before; and its influence, from the example it set in its construction and day-to-day working, was profound. As the first chapter of this book shows, it had great difficulties to contend with, in projection, building, and operation. Not all of those were overcome successfully. Its locomotives were by no means uniformly efficient. Despite the glamour of the opening day, for a time it dropped out of the business of carrying passengers – leaving that to contractors, who were allowed to work on the line with coaches drawn not by locomotives but by horses, working singly.

Five years later a much bigger undertaking began to operate, the Liverpool & Manchester Railway, which was worked mechanically throughout and set itself resolutely to the task of conveying passengers. It is often hailed as the first complete railway in the world – the first, that is, that combined, and used consistently from the outset, all the essential elements of the modern railway.

The claim is justified, and yet the Liverpool & Manchester owed much to the Stockton & Darlington. That was no secret. It sent deputations to study the older railway, and at every point we can see it learning by what the Stockton & Darlington company had done before it. Looking back over the whole history of railways, one returns always to the Stockton & Darlington for its achievement, sometimes for its failures, for the example it set to the world.

The original company formed in 1821 had an independent life of over 40 years, until it came to merge with the North Eastern in 1863. Ken Hoole has reviewed that history here, to show us something of the way in which a private company worked in the early days of public railway transport.

In the second chapter I sketch the development of railways in Britain as a whole during private ownership, from 1825 to 1947: the growth of the system, one of the densest in the world, its developing technology, the social changes it helped to bring about. Then Michael Bonavia takes over, and in the third chapter he recounts the story of the British railways since they were nationalised. He shows us some of the problems and the opportunities brought by public ownership and discusses the performance of the railways, often in adverse conditions, their achievements and at some points their failures.

Finally, Ian Waller takes the railways as they are today and helps us to look forward to what is to come. Where are they going? What services do they render, and what new services may they hope to render over the next 10 or 15 years?

This is a book about the past, the present, and the future. It takes an organism first demonstrated to the world in 1825 and shows how it has grown, contracted, changed, to become the British Railways we know today: vigorously alive, and facing new situations ahead, as railways have done for the past 150 years.

Although the British Railways Board has co-operated in the production of this book, the contributors have been left free to express their own opinions. They do not in any sense represent the Board's policy.

12 December 1974   JACK SIMMONS

1. The Stockton & Darlington Railway

In 1975 celebrations are being held to commemorate the 150th anniversary of the opening of the world's first steam-worked public railway. Public railways had been built before 1825, usually with horses as the motive power, although gravity was often utilised, and in some parts of the country, notably in north-eastern England, steam traction had been in use for some years. These very early locomotives were generally put to work hauling wagons of coal, and as the coal and the railway were usually owned by one man, or a company, the railway was not available for use by the public. The Stockton & Darlington Railway, however, could be used by anyone, on payment of the appropriate charges, either to convey goods in his own wagons, paying the railway company a toll for the use of the track and other facilities, or to have goods conveyed in wagons owned by the railway company, which also provided the motive power. It provided for the conveyance of passengers on its opening day, and shortly afterwards in regular service.

A few Stockton & Darlington locomotives and coaches have survived, and there are still plenty of earthworks – cuttings and embankments – as well as bridges, and the sites of long-vanished lines, to be seen scattered about the southern half of County Durham, particularly in the Shildon area. The original

See Plate 5

engine, *Locomotion*, built by Robert Stephenson & Co. in 1825, has been preserved since 1857, set first on a plinth outside North Road station at Darlington, and since 1892 under cover at the main-line Bank Top station, also at Darlington. When early in 1856 *Locomotion* was deemed unfit for further use, it was included in a batch of old Stockton & Darlington engines which were advertised for sale at an auction to be held at Stockton on 16 January 1856. Fortunately the intrinsic value of this engine was realised in time and it was withdrawn from the sale and restored to something resembling its original condition. During its working life this engine had undergone a number of alterations and it is doubtful if there is much of the original locomotive remaining. However, it gives an idea of what the engine was like when it hauled the first trainload of coal and passengers from Shildon to Stockton on 27 September 1825. Plans are in hand to transfer

See Plate 6

Locomotion (and its younger brother *Derwent*) to North Road station, which is being adapted as a museum.

It was the Stockton & Darlington's belated decision to preserve this pioneer locomotive that started a chain of events which culminated in 1975 with the celebrations marking the 150th anniversary of the line. When the Stockton & Darlington was taken over by the North Eastern Railway, it continued to be run by a separate Committee, and this Committee suggested that suitable celebrations should be held in 1875 to mark the 50th anniversary of the opening, to which the NER directors agreed. The event was marked by a display of old and

See Plate 10

new locomotives held at North Road Locomotive Works at Darlington, and by the unveiling of a statue to Joseph Pease, the first railway treasurer, also at Darlington. The town itself was gaily decorated for the occasion.

When the centenary came along in 1925 the London & North Eastern Railway staged an even more ambitious display of locomotives, beginning with a procession of 53 old and new engines from Stockton to Darlington over the course of the original line of 1825, followed by a large static display of locomotives, rolling stock, relics, and documents, at the new Faverdale wagon works in Darlington. This event received world-wide publicity and it is still well remembered in north-eastern England.

Recognition should also be given to the officers of the NER, notably J. B. Harper, who collected together so many old items of railway interest in the 30 or so years prior to 1925. They rescued numerous pieces of railway equipment which dated back to the earliest days of railways but which, at the turn of the century, were being superseded and scrapped. These objects were stored at York and after forming part of the Centenary display at Faverdale in 1925 they formed the nucleus of the collection at the Railway Museum at York, so long looked after by E. M. Bywell as a labour of love. Now work is in hand to provide a National Railway Museum at York, covering the history of all the public railways of Great Britain, but the parts played by the Stockton & Darlington, the North Eastern, and the London & North Eastern in preserving much of our first railways must not be forgotten.

The Stockton & Darlington Railway did not run only between the two towns mentioned in its title. Certainly the eastern terminus was at Stockton originally (later moved further east to Middlesbrough, then Redcar, and finally Saltburn), but the western terminus was some 12 miles north-west of Darlington at Witton Park colliery, near Low Etherley. Originally Darlington played only a small part in the actual operation of the railway, although its offices were located there. The main centre of operations was Shildon, where the locomotive headquarters were established from the very beginning of the railway, largely because it was at Shildon, at the foot of Brusselton incline, that rope haulage ceased and locomotives took over the haulage of the trains to Stockton. In fact it was not until 1863, when North Road Locomotive Works were opened, that Darlington began to play a larger part in the Stockton & Darlington operation. This then led to the decline of Shildon. The locomotive works there closed in 1871; however, a wagon building works was established on the site of the old locomotive works, and in the 1930s the running sheds were incorporated in the wagon works. Since then the wagon works have flourished, still helping to build and maintain the wagon fleet owned by British Railways.

Darlington was the headquarters of the Company from the very beginning and, as is well known, the impetus for the formation and early development of the concern largely came from the Pease family, which owned woollen mills in the town, even though the original suggestion for a railway appears to have come from Stockton. The Pease family not only provided some of the capital for the railway but also played a very large part in its management. It was Edward Pease who persuaded the Committee to accept George Stephenson's survey, and he also pinned his faith on the steam locomotive, leading to the granting of powers in the 1823 Act to use locomotive engines on the railway. Successive generations took part in railway management and the name Pease appeared on the Boards of many companies right through to the London & North Eastern, giving more than a century of service to railways.

The Making of the Railway

In the eighteenth century, and the early part of the nineteenth, the small coal mines in south-west Durham had difficulty in getting their coal to the centres of population such as Stockton and Darlington, and to the coast where it could be shipped to London, or exported. For many years a canal was discussed; a survey was sponsored in 1768. However, nothing was done until September 1810 when, at a dinner held in Stockton to mark the opening of a diversion of the River Tees, improved transport facilities to the west were discussed and it was suggested that a canal or a railway might be the answer.

A Committee was formed to investigate the possibilities but it was unable to decide which would best suit the needs, and John Rennie was asked to make a survey. When he made his report in August 1813 he came out in favour of a canal. However, at this time there were two factions, one favouring a route serving Darlington, and the other a more direct route: Christopher Tennant preferred the latter course and he financed another survey, this time carried out by George Leather.

At about this time the limited success of the steam locomotive was making news. William Chapman, William Hedley, and George Stephenson were striving for success on Tyneside, whilst John Blenkinsop and Matthew Murray introduced steam locomotives on the Middleton Railway (near Leeds) in 1812. Blenkinsop locomotives were also used in Northumberland in 1813.

Tennant's suggestion regarding a canal direct from the coalfield to Stockton spurred the citizens of Darlington and Yarm to action, for they wanted any canal or railway that was built to serve their towns. Consequently in 1818 yet another survey was carried out, this time by a Welsh engineer named George Overton, with the brief to find the most suitable route for a railway serving, of course, both Darlington and Yarm.

However, before Darlington could gather support, the Mayor of Stockton called a meeting on 31 July 1818 at which the main speaker was Leonard Raisbeck, solicitor to the Tees Navigation Company; the Chairman was the Earl of Strathmore. Estimates of the cost of a canal and the possible receipts were presented to the large body of supporters gathered in the Town Hall and resolutions were passed supporting the scheme, urging immediate application to Parliament for the necessary powers.

Stockton's enthusiasm for a direct canal did not satisfy Darlington and Yarm, which stood the chance of being left out in the cold. A number of influential men lived in the old market town of Yarm – Thomas Meynell, Benjamin Flounders, Richard Miles, and Jonathan Backhouse – and Thomas Meynell's agent, Jeremiah

Cairns, was connected by marriage with Overton. On being approached for his comments on the superiority of a canal or a railway, Overton favoured a railway, and he was asked if he would travel north to County Durham to carry out yet another survey, which he started on 3 September. In the meantime the Darlington and Yarm groups had got together and meetings were held in Darlington on 17 August and 4 September 1818 to discuss the scheme.

At the latter meeting the main topic was again the advantages of a canal or a railway, and their probable routes, but a great step forward was made when resolutions were passed authorising the Committee to look into the building of a railway from Stockton to the collieries, or a canal from Stockton to Darlington and a railway from Darlington to the collieries.

Overton completed his survey on 20 September 1818, proving that a canal was feasible from Stockton to Darlington, and also plotting the line of a railway from Stockton to Etherley, the latter costing an estimated £124,000 but including branches to Croft, Yarm, and Piercebridge. In the meantime the necessary Parliamentary notices had appeared and it was essential that a full application should be made to Parliament before 30 September. Unfortunately the plans were prepared in such a hurry that they were found to be incomplete and the Bill was rejected. However, in the meantime further meetings had been held in Darlington and on 31 October the results to date were placed before a meeting in Stockton. On 13 November a very important meeting was held at Darlington, when the canal or railway controversy was finally settled and it was decided to go ahead with an application to Parliament for powers to build "A TRAMWAY".

On the basis of the decisions taken at this meeting a prospectus was issued, drawn up by Joseph Pease at the age of 19! The estimated cost of the line had been reduced to £113,000 and the annual receipts were estimated to bring in £16,500 a year. Within a week £25,000 had been subscribed. The largest subscribers were Thomas Meynell, Jonathan Backhouse, William Chaytor, Jeremiah Cairns, Edward Pease, Joseph Gurney, Thomas Richardson, and Benjamin Flounders. Other names in the list, who were later to become famous, were John Kitching, William Kitching Jnr, and Joseph Pease.

The Bill was again rejected, this time by 106 votes to 93, but almost immediately the Committee decided to continue with its efforts to get the Bill through Parliament, only to be delayed by the death of George III (which involved a dissolution and a general election) on 29 January 1820. At a meeting held in Yarm on 12 February it was decided to postpone operations and thus the new Bill did not receive attention until the 1820–1 session. This time, its route modified by Overton and with opposition circumscribed, it passed through the various stages and thus became an Act when it received the Royal Assent on 19 April 1821.

The Act authorised "making and maintaining a Railway or Tramroad from the River Tees at Stockton, to Witton Park Colliery, with several Branches therefrom, all in the County of Durham". The branches were to the Darlington Depots; the Black Boy branch from Shildon to Coundon; the Norlees House (now North

Leazes) to Evenwood Lane branch; the Yarm branch; and a branch at Stockton. The Company was empowered to erect bridges, piers, arches, tunnels, aqueducts, basins, wharfs, houses, warehouses, toll houses, landing places, weighing beams, cranes, fire engines, or other machines. The maximum rates to be charged were stipulated, including additional rates payable on goods which had to traverse the inclined planes. Privately-owned wagons were allowed on the line and they had to have the name or names of the owner(s), places of abode, and the number of the vehicle, registered with the company, and each wagon or coach had to carry "the name and number in large White capital Letters and Figures on a Black ground, Three inches high at the least and a proportionate breadth on some conspicuous part of the outside". Any landowner within five miles of the line was entitled to connect his own branch with the Stockton & Darlington line if he so wished. Altogether the Act ran to 67 pages.

By this time Edward Pease was taking a great interest in the project, favouring a railway for the whole distance between the collieries and Stockton and passing, of course, near to Darlington, where his woollen mills would benefit from the reduction in the price of coal, and transport generally. Pease had heard of George Stephenson's activities on Tyneside, 40 miles to the north, and a meeting between the two was arranged for 19 April 1821, the day the first Act was passed.

On returning home, and after thinking about his discussion with Edward Pease, Stephenson wrote saying that he would be happy to be of service, but that he could not devote the whole of his time to the railway. He was willing to undertake a survey within the limits of the Act of Parliament and he recommended that the whole of the work involved in building the line should be carried out by contractors.

At the first meeting of the shareholders of the newly-formed company on 12 May 1821, Edward Pease and Thomas Meynell were authorised to approach various engineers regarding the construction of the line. These included Robert Stevenson of Edinburgh and George Stephenson of Killingworth, and the outcome was that the latter was engaged to make a further survey. Edward Pease was obviously in favour of Stephenson and on 28 July he wrote to him asking what the cost of the survey would be. A significant stipulation was that the line should "remain as long as any coal in the district remains", for the working-out of the mines in north-west Durham has since led to the closure of many lines in the area, including the original course of the Stockton & Darlington from Shildon to Witton Park.

Stephenson received instructions on 15 October 1821 to begin his survey, and in this he was assisted by his son Robert, then aged 18. They were accompanied by John Dixon, a native of the area, who was later to assist Stephenson with the Liverpool & Manchester Railway, and in particular the building of the line across Chat Moss. He eventually returned to County Durham in the employ of the Stockton & Darlington Railway and became the Company's Engineer.

Stephenson's survey was completed before the end of 1821, deviating from Overton's line at various points, notably near Darlington, where Stephenson

brought the line even nearer the northern edge of the town before turning north
to Simpasture.

At long last things began to move. George Stephenson presented his report on
18 January 1822 and four days later he was appointed Engineer at £660 per
annum. Materials were ordered, contractors were employed to construct the line,
and on 23 May the first rails were ceremonially laid at St John's Crossing, Stockton, by Thomas Meynell, the Chairman of the Company. From Stockton to
Darlington the earthworks were light, the land being almost level, and on this
section the rails were laid on oak blocks shipped from Portsea to Stockton; north
of Darlington stone blocks were used. Fish-bellied rails of malleable iron weighing 28lb. per yard were preferred to cast-iron rails because of their greater
strength: these were $2\frac{1}{4}$ in. wide on top, with a depth of 2 in. at each end and
$3\frac{1}{4}$ in. in the middle, thus giving the fish-bellied shape. They were of two lengths,
12 ft. and 15 ft. The cast-iron chairs weighed 6lb. each and they were set $\frac{1}{2}$ in.
into the stone blocks and fixed by two spikes. The stone blocks were usually
about 18 in. square and 10 in. to 12 in. deep and the initial order was for
64,000. The oak blocks were 20 in. by 6 in. and 6 in. to 8 in. deep.

Stephenson's alterations were included in the second Act, obtained on 23 May
1823. Perhaps its most important clause was that authorising the use of steam
power and the carriage of passengers, although the significance of these provisions
was not realised at the time. The actual wording was as follows:

> That it shall be lawful for the Company of Proprietors to make and erect
> such and so many loco-motive or moveable Engines, as the said Company
> shall from time to time think proper and expedient, and to use and employ
> the same in or upon the said Railways or Tramroads or any of them, for the
> purpose of facilitating the transport conveyance and carriage of Goods, Mer-
> chandize and other articles and things upon and along the same Roads, and
> for the conveyance of Passengers upon and along the same Roads.

As a result of obtaining these powers, Robert Stephenson & Co. were
approached on 16 July 1824 regarding the supply of steam locomotives, and
on 16 September it was agreed that they should build two engines at £500 each.
Also in 1824 a start was made on two of the most important bridges – the stone
bridge over the Skerne on the northern outskirts of Darlington (which is still in
use) and the cast-iron bridge over the Gaunless at West Auckland (which was
replaced in 1900–1). The third Act of 17 May 1824 amended the route of the
branch to Evenwood Lane and transformed it into the Haggerleases branch.

Throughout 1824 work went on slowly, but when the first locomotive was
delivered on 16 September 1825 the line was in a sufficient state of readiness to
enable it to be opened, and on the following day notices were posted to the
effect that there would be a grand opening on Tuesday 27 September. In the
meantime the one and only locomotive had been steamed: in fact, after it had
been delivered by road to Aycliffe Lane (later Heighington) on 16 September,
steam was raised to enable it to be worked to Shildon under its own power. It is

said that the fire was kindled by the power of the sun's rays focused through a magnifying glass onto a pile of wooden shavings.

The Railway in Being

The opening ceremony was an event of great excitement in the district and crowds of spectators turned out to watch the steam locomotive haul its trainload of passengers and goods on its very first trip from Shildon to Stockton. Some of the wagons of coal had started their journey at Phoenix Pit at the northern extremity of the line, whence they were drawn up the Etherley north bank by the winding engine at the summit. Down the south side of the ridge it was possible to work the incline on the self-acting principle as the loaded wagons were running down-hill. The self-acting method of working on inclines can only be used where the gradient is in favour of the load, as it is usual to balance the empty wagons ascending the incline by a similar number of wagons descending. The contents of the descending wagons then have to be sufficient to overcome the force of gravity acting on the ascending wagons. By this method power is saved and an even flow of wagons is ensured.

From the foot of the Etherley south incline the wagons were hauled by horses across the level stretch to the foot of the Brusselton north incline, where they were attached to the rope worked by the winding engine at the summit. Shortly after leaving the foot of Etherley bank at St Helens Auckland, the line crossed the handsome cast-iron bridge across the River Gaunless, the first iron railway bridge in the world. This had been designed by George Stephenson and it was cast in Newcastle; the parts were then transported to the site and the bridge was erected. At first there were three spans, but floods in the winter of 1823–4 damaged the bridge and a fourth span was added before the line was opened.

In 1900 a new colliery was planned south of the Gaunless and as it was necessary for locomotives to cross the river the old bridge was replaced. Fortunately it was carefully dismantled and the parts were stored for many years at Darlington before the bridge eventually found a resting place in the Railway Museum at York.

On the Brusselton north bank there are still a number of stone sleepers, and there is also a handsome small bridge to allow a farmer to get from one side of the line to the other. At Brusselton bank top the outline of the engine house can still be seen in the stones of a cottage, and from this point it is possible to look down the final incline to Masons Arms level crossing, where the wagons were coupled to the first locomotive for their journey to Stockton.

The programme for the opening day stated that the inaugural train would be made up of

6 wagons with coal and merchandise
The Committee in the Company's coach
6 wagons fitted with seats
14 wagons for the conveyance of workmen
6 wagons of coal (to be detached at Darlington)

1   Opening of the Stockton & Darlington Railway, 27 Sept. 1825. From a sketch by
John Dobbin, made some time after the event.

Crowds of people turned out to watch the inaugural train on the opening day
and tickets were issued to about 300 people. However, there was such a crowd
that it became a free-for-all and people clambered on to the wagons to obtain a ride.

People on foot and on horseback tried to race the train, which on the gradually
falling gradient towards Darlington frequently reached 12 m.p.h., and at one
place 15 m.p.h. Darlington, $8\frac{3}{4}$ miles from Shildon, was reached in 65 minutes,
exclusive of stops, and there six wagons of coal were detached. After taking on
board a band, and after the engine had obtained a further supply of water, the
train set off for Stockton. This part of the journey, nearly 12 miles, took 3 hours
and 7 minutes inclusive of stops.

One contemporary account states that there were between 550 and 600 people
in, and on top of, the wagons, with a number clinging to the sides, making the
load about 80 tons. It went on:

Nothing could exceed the beauty and grandeur of the scene. Throughout the
whole distance the fields and lanes were covered with elegantly-dressed

females, and all descriptions of spectators. The bridges under which the procession in some places darted with such astonishing rapidity, lined with spectators cheering and waving their hats, had a grand effect. At Darlington the whole inhabitants of the town were out to witness the procession.

But though all along the line people on foot crowded the fields on each side, and here and there a lady or gentleman on horseback, yet the procession was not joined by many horses and carriages until it approached within a few miles of Stockton; and here the situation of the Rail-way, which runs parallel and close to the turnpike road leading to Yarm and Stockton, gave them a fine opportunity of viewing the procession. Numerous horses, carriages, gigs, carts, and other vehicles travelled along with the engine, and her immense train of carriages, in some places within a few yards, without the horses seeming the least frightened; and at one time the passengers by the engine had the pleasure of accompanying and cheering their brother passengers by the stage coach, which passed alongside, and of observing the striking contrast exhibited by the power of the engine and of horses; the engine with her six hundred passengers and load, and the coach with four horses, and only sixteen passengers.

On arrival at Stockton the train was welcomed by a salute of guns, and cheers from the waiting crowd, and the locomotive and wagons were inspected by a wondering multitude as the triumphant directors, the guests, and the workmen went off for a well-earned meal.

Although George Stephenson was the Engineer, his services were soon in demand in many places where a railway was under consideration, and the task of keeping the locomotives running fell on Timothy Hackworth. He had gained experience of steam locomotives on Tyneside and he was appointed Locomotive Foreman in May 1825, some four months before the delivery of the first engine. His starting salary was £150 a year, with a free house and free coal, and in addition to maintaining the locomotives he was responsible for the wagons and winding engines. As the fleet of locomotives grew larger, he had to devise ways and means of repairing them, using the primitive tools of the day and with little accommodation. From these small beginnings he built up the locomotive works at Shildon, where all Stockton & Darlington engines were maintained and overhauled until the new North Road Works at Darlington opened on 1 January 1863. New machinery and room for expansion at Darlington meant the decline of Shildon, and locomotive building ceased there in 1867; four years later the locomotive repair work was also transferred to Darlington.

The railway was run with strong personal contact between the directors and the staff. Anyone breaking the rules was given a fatherly lecture by Edward Pease, and perhaps fined a small amount. Of course in those days the staff and the public were used to the leisurely pace of a horse and it took them some time to adjust to the fact that the locomotives could travel much faster than a horse and, with a heavy coal train behind them, could not stop as quickly as a horse-drawn vehicle.

At last the line was open and traffic started to flow, worked mostly by horses because at the time of opening the company possessed only one engine. The line was single, with passing loops, and regulations were issued laying down the priority to be given to various types of traffic. Passenger traffic was not at first envisaged, but shortly after the opening it was decided to operate such services and the necessary licence was applied for on 7 October 1825. At the same time the company provided a coach for the passenger service and this, named *Experiment*, began running on 10 October. The fare for the journey from Stockton to Darlington was a shilling, and the coach ran in both directions on four days of the week, and in one direction only on the other two; there was no Sunday service. On Mondays the coach ran from Stockton to Darlington and back; on Tuesdays it ran from Stockton to Darlington; on Wednesdays, Thursdays, and Fridays from Darlington to Stockton and back; and on Saturdays from Darlington to Stockton. The time taken for the journey was two hours, a distance of almost 12 miles.

On the following day, 11 October, the Yarm branch was opened to coal traffic, and six days later the depots were complete and ready for use. The railway company's terminus was actually at Egglescliffe, on the north bank of the River Tees, but its object was to serve the old market town of Yarm, just across the river. The regular passenger service to Yarm was discontinued from 7 September 1833, when steam locomotives began working the passenger trains between Darlington and Stockton. To save these trains running along the branch, and then having to reverse back to the junction, they stopped at Yarm Branch End station, situated at the junction of the branch with the main line. However, horse-drawn coaches continued to run to Yarm on the occasion of Yarm Fair.

After running the horse-drawn passenger coaches for a few months, the Stockton & Darlington decided to let this sphere of operation to contractors, and the working of the coach *Experiment* was conceded for £200 a year to Richard Pickersgill, who took it over on 1 April 1826. By this date the journey time had been reduced to 75 minutes, and a cheap fare of 9d. was payable by passengers travelling outside the coach. This proved so successful that additional seats had to be fitted and it is recorded that on one day as many as 158 passengers were carried, although it is not stated how many return journeys were made.

Over the next seven years the passenger traffic developed beyond the Company's expectations, so that when they decided to operate the passenger trains with steam locomotives from 7 September 1833, the coach proprietors had to be bought out at a cost of £316 17s 8d. However, the average daily receipt from the coaches was only £7 10s 0d.

At Darlington the coaches started from a point near the Great North Road, and at the Stockton end they terminated on the river bank at Stockton Wharf, not far from the High Street. Intermediately passengers were picked up or set down where they signalled the coach to stop, but it became the practice for passengers to wait at some of the inns near the railway, and the name of one of these – Fighting Cocks – remains in railway use to this very day.

The coal depots at Darlington, where the coal was unloaded from the railway wagons for sale to the inhabitants, were at the end of a short branch which diverged from the Stockton & Darlington main line near to where the present North Road station stands. The coal cells, where the coal was stored, were close to the North Road, making for easy distribution, but they became disused in 1872 when new depots were opened at Hill House. The land on which the old depots were built was sold, but some of the original walls can still be located.

Meanwhile at Shildon four cottages had been authorised on 30 September 1825. Hackworth was busy keeping the one locomotive in working order and preparing for the arrival of the second engine, which was delivered from Robert Stephenson & Co. on 1 November. The site chosen for the buildings to house the locomotives was at the foot of Brusselton Incline and as the works developed so did the number of cottages for the workmen, and the area became known as New Shildon, to distinguish it from the original village a short distance to the north. Eventually the two communities were joined. Two more engines were delivered by Stephenson & Co. in 1826, No. 3 *Black Diamond* on 17 April and No. 4 *Diligence* on 18 May, at a cost of £600 each. It should be emphasised, however, that originally the engines carried neither names nor numbers and these were not introduced until 1827.

Henceforward the Stockton & Darlington gradually built up its locomotive stock and although there were times of crisis, when most of the engines were laid up for repairs, there was no question of the haulage being taken over completely by horses. Figures show that the engines were able to haul more wagons than the horses and could complete the round trip from Shildon to Stockton and back in less time. In fact at a Committee Meeting held at the George Hotel in Yarm on 10 July 1827 it was reported that "as a result of a strict scrutiny into the subject there appears to be a saving of nearly 30 per cent in favour of haulage performed by Locomotive Engines when compared with its being done by horses".

Although locomotives continued to be ordered from contractors right up to the end of the Stockton & Darlington Railway, numerous engines were built at Shildon Works by Hackworth, and his successor William Bouch. However, Hackworth's first engine was one which incorporated parts from a locomotive purchased by the company but which had proved unsuccessful.

Using the boiler, which had been lengthened, Hackworth produced the *Royal George*, an engine with six coupled wheels, which proved ideal for working the mineral trains to Stockton and the empty wagons back again. Eventually the majority of locomotives owned by the Stockton & Darlington were of the six-coupled type, although considerably different from Hackworth's pioneer engine.

In 1833 the company decided to let out to contract the work of driving and maintaining the locomotives, the largest contractor being Timothy Hackworth, who continued to use Shildon Works where he had, until then, been an employee. Now that he was no longer employed by the Stockton & Darlington he was able to expand his private business interests and he built his own locomotive works at Soho, on the outskirts of Shildon. The new works were run by his brother, Thomas, whilst Timothy was engaged on Stockton & Darlington matters, but undoubtedly Timothy was behind the developments at Soho, where locomotives were built for railways in many different parts of the world.

The other two contractors were W. & A. Kitching and William Lister, who both had premises at Hopetown, Darlington, adjacent to the present North Road station.

To accommodate the passengers at Darlington when the steam-worked service was introduced in September 1833, the company decided on 23 August to convert the goods warehouse into "a place convenient for passengers waiting to take the Railway Coaches". One of the staff at Darlington and Stockton was to be responsible for seeing that passenger trains were started, presumably on time. In November 1833 part of the coach station at Darlington was converted into a shop and dwelling house. These were let to Mary Simpson at £5 a year for twelve months on condition that "she kept the coach office clean and afforded every necessary accommodation to coach passengers".

By 1833 the stock of locomotives had risen to 23, but the line was still little more than a mineral line conveying coal from the collieries to Stockton and Middlesbrough. In the first eight years of its existence the Stockton & Darlington had constructed the Black Boy branch to serve a colliery of that name north of Shildon, opened in 1827; the Croft branch southwards from Darlington to serve coal depots near Croft Bridge, opened on 27 September 1829; the Haggerleases branch westwards from St Helens (later known as West Auckland) to serve several coal mines along the Gaunless valley; and the Middlesbrough branch eastwards from Stockton, along the south bank of the River Tees, to Middlesbrough, where it was intended to develop a new town and improved coal shipping facilities.

A horse-drawn passenger coach was introduced on the Croft branch when it opened but the service was withdrawn on 13 December 1833, although the coal depots at the end of the branch continued in use until 27 April 1964. The Haggerleases branch (opened 1 October 1830) developed into a hive of activity as small mines sprang up on either side of the Gaunless valley. The branch carried a passenger service between 1858 and 1872 but this ran only as far as Lands, except for a period in 1859 when it ran through to Haggerleases. The terminus at Haggerleases was renamed Butterknowle from 1 September 1899, and the goods service was withdrawn on 30 September 1963, although a truncated service to the foot of Randolph Colliery incline ran until August 1968.

The most important development by far in the early years of the Stockton & Darlington Railway was the Middlesbrough branch. Soon after the opening of the line it had been found that Stockton Wharf was not entirely suitable as a shipping place for the coal coming down the line. In spite of a number of improvements carried out on the river (it will be remembered that the dinner held at Stockton in October 1810 when a railway was first mooted was to mark one of these schemes), it was still a hazardous journey because of the shallows liable to be encountered, and it was obvious that if shipment could take place further downstream then larger vessels could be used.

The site chosen was at Middlesbrough, east of Stockton, but on the opposite bank of the Tees, where in the 1820s there was only a small population farming the low-lying land. With a view to developing the area generally, land was purchased by a consortium known as the Middlesbrough Owners, in which the Pease family played a large part. A shipping place was soon established and a competition for the best design of coal drops for loading the coal into ships was won by Timothy Hackworth. The branch to serve the new port – it was originally known as Port Darlington – crossed the River Tees on a suspension bridge shortly after striking off the 1825 line to St Johns Crossing at Stockton. Unfortunately the bridge proved to be unsuccessful and loads over it were severely limited until a more substantial bridge could be built.

However, from these small beginnings Middlesbrough eventually grew into a thriving town, full of heavy industry, with a supply of ironstone on its very doorstep, and the Stockton & Darlington ready to carry the coal and limestone needed to produce iron in quantity. The development of the ironstone industry in the Eston and Cleveland Hills is a story in its own right – how the various mines and drifts grew, expanded, failed, re-opened as trade improved, and finally closed for good. Although Middlesbrough is still an important iron and steel producing centre, the whole of the ore used is imported from abroad: not a single ounce of ironstone is produced from the nearby mines which at one time were busy and booming but are now derelict and disused.

After shipping coal from the drops on the river bank, the Middlesbrough Owners decided to build a dock at Middlesbrough and this was opened on 12 May 1842, with an area of nine acres and accommodation for some 150 small ships of the period. The owners had the sole right to ship coal east of Stockton, and to serve the dock they built a branch line from the Stockton & Darlington.

The dock became the focal point for the coal traffic of the Stockton & Darlington, and it was enlarged in 1874. Its importance continued until well into the twentieth century and it is only recently that deep-water berths have been provided nearer the mouth of the River Tees to accommodate larger vessels. In fact the North Eastern Railway found the traffic of sufficient importance to warrant the electrification of the line from Shildon to Middlesbrough, which was completed in 1915. The route chosen was part Stockton & Darlington (Shildon to Simpasture Junction and Bowesfield Junction to Erimus Yard); part Clarence Railway (Simpasture Junction to Carlton West Junction); and part North Eastern (Carlton West Junction to Bowesfield Junction). This avoided the crossing on the level of the East Coast main line at Darlington as the Clarence route bridged the main line near Aycliffe.

After the Stockton & Darlington Railway had been formed, and it was decided that the line should run via Darlington and Yarm, the Clarence Railway was promoted by the faction which preferred a direct route from Stockton to the coalfield.

The Clarence Railway actually connected with the Stockton & Darlington at Simpasture Junction, and with its shorter route could offer lower rates for coal traffic to Teesside. Naturally this was not to the liking of the Stockton & Darlington Company and it imposed extra tolls to keep the traffic on its own line.

Extensions North, East, and West

After the opening of the Stockton to Middlesbrough line in December 1830, the Stockton & Darlington Railway expanded very little in its own right and, except for minor improvements and connecting lines, it was another 30 years before the company carried out any major extensions. This is not to say that the line did not expand, but the company preferred to finance its extensions through separate concerns, each one constituted to build a specific branch or length of line consistent with Stockton & Darlington needs. Thus the extensions were carried out by the following companies:

Northwards

Bishop Auckland & Weardale Railway	Shildon to Crook
Wear Valley Railway	Wear Valley Junction to Frosterley
Frosterley & Stanhope Railway	Frosterley to Stanhope

Westwards

Darlington & Barnard Castle Railway	Darlington (Hopetown Junction) to Barnard Castle
South Durham & Lancashire Union Railway	Bishop Auckland–Barnard Castle–Kirkby Stephen–Tebay
Eden Valley Railway	Kirkby Stephen to Clifton

Eastwards

| Middlesbrough & Redcar Railway | Middlesbrough to Redcar |
| Middlesbrough & Guisborough Railway | Middlesbrough to Guisborough |

In addition the strategic Shildon Tunnel was built privately and sold to the Stockton & Darlington for £223,450 in 1847, five years after its opening. It is approximately 1,220 yds. long and is still in use, although now carrying only a single track instead of the two tracks for which it was built. This tunnel passes through the barrier of high land north of Shildon and it gave access not only to Bishop Auckland, but also to Crook and Weardale, opening up further rich mineral-producing areas. The new route through Shildon tunnel eventually replaced the original line over the Brusselton inclines, and thus the heavy traffic from the Gaunless valley could be locomotive-worked throughout. However, the two inclines serving Etherley were still necessary, but as access to the area was also provided by the Bishop Auckland & Weardale line to Crook the importance of the original 1825 route was rapidly fading.

The partners in the Shildon Tunnel Company were Joseph Pease, Thomas Meynell, and Henry Stobart, all directors of the Stockton & Darlington Railway, and of numerous other railway concerns in the north-east. Between them they were on the boards of seven railway companies in the area.

In addition to the Stockton & Darlington directors, the boards of the various companies usually contained a sprinkling of local industrialists, local land-owners or nobility, and by this "old boys' network" the company had little difficulty in getting its schemes financed and authorised. It was only when it came up against the interests of the North Eastern Railway or the thorn-in-the-side West Hartlepool Harbour & Railway that trouble arose.

BISHOP AUCKLAND & WEARDALE

Authorised on 15 July 1837 to build a line from Shildon to Witton-le-Wear, with a branch from Wear Valley Junction to Crook, in the event the line consisted of part of the main line from Shildon to Wear Valley Junction, and the branch to Crook, leaving the section between Wear Valley Junction and Witton-le-Wear in abeyance, although it was built later by another company. The Bishop Auckland & Weardale branched off the Stockton & Darlington's 1825 line at Soho, adjacent to the present Shildon station, and after passing through Shildon Tunnel reached South Church on 19 April 1842. Here a small station was erected and it served as the terminus of the line until the remaining portion of the line as far as Crook was opened on 8 November 1843. For a period from 1 May 1842 a horse-bus service was run between South Church and the southern terminus of the Durham Junction Railway at Rainton Meadows, there being at that date no through connection by rail. South Church remained in use after the line had been pushed forward to Bishop Auckland and Crook and is believed to have closed in 1845, although it was not actually demolished until a few years ago.

When the line was opened to Crook it simply passed through Bishop Auckland without any connections, but with the coming of the North Eastern branch from Leamside and Durham in 1857 the station began to grow into an important and busy centre, culminating in a station having a triangular layout, with a platform on each of the three inside faces and on one of the outside faces. The opening of a connecting line from Bishop Auckland to Fieldon Bridge Junction on 1 August 1863 created a through route from north-east Durham to Westmorland, Cumberland, and the Barrow area of Lancashire.

Immediately north of Crook the Pease family built up a large complex of coal mines, coke ovens, brickworks, etc., and thus provided a large amount of traffic for the line in which they had such a great interest.

WEAR VALLEY AND FROSTERLEY & STANHOPE

The Wear Valley Railway was authorised on 31 July 1845, traversing from Wear Valley Junction to Witton-le-Wear the course planned but not built by the Bishop Auckland & Weardale Railway. However, the Wear Valley extended beyond Witton-le-Wear and it was opened throughout to Frosterley on 3 August

1847. The line served rich limestone deposits in the Bishopley area, east of Frosterley, where the Stockton & Darlington established large quarries and lime-kilns, although they were usually operated by contractors. To serve more large quarries further up the Wear valley, an extension from Frosterley to Stanhope was authorised on 28 June 1861 and opened on 22 October 1862. Although really outside the scope of this section it may be mentioned that the line was extended even further along the valley to Wearhead under the powers of the Wear Valley Extension Act of 20 June 1892. This additional nine-mile stretch was opened on 21 October 1895.

DARLINGTON & BARNARD CASTLE

This line was built as a result of the citizens of Barnard Castle pressing for rail connection with the Stockton & Darlington line. As early as 1832 a deputation from Barnard Castle was received by the Stockton & Darlington directors, but no agreement was reached and it was not until a second meeting in 1852 that progress was made. However, some difficulty was encountered when the embryo company wished to cross land owned by the Duke of Cleveland, and the first Bill was thrown out in 1853 after ten days before a Select Committee in Parliament. A second Bill, with a modified route, was more successful, and on 3 July 1854 the Royal Assent was received. The first sod was cut only 16 days later, and the line was completed and opened on 8 July 1856. It branched off the Stockton & Darlington line at Hopetown Junction, north-west of North Road station in Darlington, and ran parallel to the River Tees for much of the way to Barnard Castle, crossing the river twice between Gainford and Winston.

SOUTH DURHAM & LANCASHIRE UNION RAILWAY

The largest project tackled by any Stockton & Darlington subsidiary was the South Durham & Lancashire Union line from Spring Gardens Junction (near West Auckland), through Barnard Castle and Kirkby Stephen, to Tebay in Westmorland. This involved building a line across much wild and inhospitable country between Barnard Castle and Kirkby Stephen, and crossing the Pennines at Stainmore summit. There was little hope of any local traffic and really the line was built to secure through traffic between the east and west coasts of England. The moorland which had to be traversed meant that there were no high costs in purchasing land, but great expense was incurred in crossing the deep, wide valleys by high and lengthy viaducts, some of stone and others of metal.

The Engineer for the line was Thomas Bouch, brother of William, the Locomotive Superintendent of the Stockton & Darlington. Thomas is remembered for his

See Plate 4 slender and graceful viaducts at Belah and Deepdale, both of all-metal construction, his stone and metal Tees viaduct just west of Barnard Castle, and the stone viaducts at Merrygill, Podgill and elsewhere along the line. Unfortunately he is even better remembered as the designer of the ill-fated Tay Bridge, which collapsed in 1879.

The South Durham line was notable for its long pull up either side of the Pennines to reach the summit at Stainmore, 1,370 ft. above sea level. Going westwards there was a 13-mile climb from Tees Valley Junction to the summit, almost half of it being at 1 in 67–9. Up the western side the climb was even more difficult, involving $2\frac{1}{2}$ miles at 1 in 59, $3\frac{1}{2}$ miles at 1 in 60, and 2 miles at 1 in 72. The line was opened in 1861.

On the Pennines the South Durham line was susceptible to heavy snowfalls and on many occasions traffic was completely halted because the line was blocked with snow. On such occasions large snowploughs were used to charge the drifts, propelled by two or sometimes three locomotives. If the snow was soft it was possible by repeated runs at it to throw it aside from the prow of the plough, but if the snow had become hard the plough could get stuck fast, or it could be derailed as the hard snow packed under the vehicle. In some cases ploughs and engines had to be abandoned for days until the weather improved. The worst occasion was in 1947 when the line was closed for weeks. Railwaymen, assisted by troops, had to dig the snow away, but an overnight wind often meant that when they arrived next morning all their previous day's work had been undone.

For years the line prospered, with Durham coke flowing westwards for the ironworks of West Cumberland and Furness, and iron ore flowing eastwards for the County Durham ironworks. The traffic was handled for the first 30 years or so by the faithful Stockton & Darlington long-boilered 0–6–0 engines, but in the last decade of the nineteenth century some of the new Worsdell compound 0–6–2T engines were drafted to the line. The most successful North Eastern class of engine to be used was the T and T1 0–8–0s, but prior to the First World War severe weight restrictions were imposed over the viaducts and the eight-coupled engines had to be replaced by the much smaller P and P1 0–6–0s.

To economise on line occupation the practice was developed of running "double loads" – the loads for two engines combined to make one train, which was then worked by two locomotives. It was also the practice for the assisting engine to be at the rear of the train over certain sections, and slip couplings were extensively used. These were special couplings with which the assisting locomotive was attached to the rear brake van of the train. When the top of the bank was reached it was possible to uncouple the banking engine from the rear of the train without stopping, by pulling a cord attached to the coupling and led back to the footplate. The coupling then parted and dropped away from the drawhook of the brake van. On a number of occasions accidents were caused when the slip coupling opened of its own accord. Unless the banking engine was kept up to the buffers of the rear van a gap opened up between the two and when the train halted the banking engine crashed into the rear. Various Board of Trade Inspecting Officers condemned the practice, but it continued until the closure of the line in 1962.

In the later stages of the line larger engines were allowed and some mineral trains were worked by three locomotives – two at the front and one at the rear. Passenger traffic never was sufficient to keep the line open, although to utilise the line to better purpose some Saturday trains connecting the north-east with Blackpool were routed over it.

EDEN VALLEY

Interested groups west of the Pennines were divided over the location of the western end of the South Durham & Lancashire Union line. Some wanted it to run up the Eden valley to join the Lancaster & Carlisle Railway south of Penrith, whilst others wanted it to run to Tebay to join the Lancaster & Carlisle there. In the end the decision was taken to run to Tebay, and therefore a new company was formed to build a line from Kirkby Stephen to Clifton, south of Penrith, running along the rich and fertile Eden valley.

When this line was opened on 8 April 1862 the connection at Clifton was such that it allowed trains to run through to the south, whereas what was needed was a route to the north. Consequently powers were immediately sought to form a new connection further north and, when this was opened on 1 August 1863, running powers were obtained over the London & North Western Railway from Eden Valley Junction to Penrith.

MIDDLESBROUGH & REDCAR

At the eastern end of the line the Middlesbrough & Redcar Railway was opened on 4 June 1846. It ran along the south bank of the Tees, originally passing through green fields, but the area on both sides of the line eventually became one of the most heavily industrialised in the north-east as ironworks spread eastwards from Middlesbrough. The new and larger works were within easy reach of the ironstone mines and drifts on the slopes of the Eston Hills and it was possible for one ironmaster to lay a line to carry the ironstone direct from the mines to the works without passing over the Stockton & Darlington.

The inaugural train from Middlesbrough to Redcar was hauled by *Locomotion* — probably the last train of passengers it pulled until it was resurrected in 1925 to work the replica train in the centenary procession. In 1846 it hauled a light train consisting of one coach (presumably carrying the Stockton & Darlington and Middlesbrough & Redcar directors) and a couple of wagons. On arrival at Redcar the foundation stone of a new station house was formally laid and the party then adjourned to the Red Lion Hotel. A special train for the general public was run from Darlington to Redcar for the occasion, conveying passengers at single fare for the return journey from any Great North of England, Newcastle & Darlington Junction, Bishop Auckland & Weardale, or Derwent Junction station. It was timed to leave Darlington at 12.15 a.m. (*sic*) and arrive at Redcar at 1.30 p.m.

At its western end the extension to Redcar used part of the line to Middlesbrough dock, which had been purchased by the Stockton & Darlington from the Middlesbrough Owners. The line from Stockton terminated in the centre of old Middlesbrough — the nucleus from which the present town has grown — and to reach the dock a branch struck off eastwards at what later became known as Old Town Junction. When eventually the Redcar extension was built, it branched off the dock line and it was at this point that a new station was built in 1847: it then became possible to run through from Darlington to Redcar without the need to reverse. The present station at Middlesbrough was built in 1877 on approximately the same site as the 1847 station.

MIDDLESBROUGH & GUISBOROUGH

Edward, Joseph, Henry, John, and Joseph Whitwell Pease were all named in the Act as subscribers to the Middlesbrough & Guisborough Railway, and Henry Pease was one of the first directors of the company, which received its Act on 17 June 1852. It branched off the Middlesbrough & Redcar line east of Middlesbrough station at what became known as Guisborough Junction, serving Ormesby, Nunthorpe, Pinchinthorpe, and Hutton Gate, before terminating at a handsome little station with an overall train-shed at Guisborough.

The Pease family had acquired ironstone-bearing land in the Codhill area south-west of Guisborough and to bring out the stone a railway was necessary. Although Guisborough was the stated objective of the line, it was planned so that a branch could easily be constructed to the Pease mines. In fact two branches were proposed. The Roseberry branch, with a total length of 2 miles 308 yds, was to run southwards from a point west of Hutton Gate station to the foot of the Cleveland Hills, then up an incline approximately 1,540 yds long at gradients of between 1 in 23 and 1 in 7½, and finally for a further mile to the mine on the crest of the hills. The latter stretch was to have included a tunnel 346 yds long, but the branch was not built.

The shorter Hutton Moor and Codhill branch, which was actually constructed, diverged at the same point as the Roseberry branch and ran in an easterly direction, again using an incline to reach the crest of the Cleveland Hills. The total length of this branch was 1 mile 76 yds but the incline was shorter (approximately 550 yds) and required easier gradients of 1 in 27 and 1 in 19.

The Middlesbrough & Guisborough Railway was opened to goods traffic on 11 November 1853, and to passenger traffic on 25 February 1854, but it closed between Nunthorpe Junction and Guisborough on 2 March 1964 (passengers) and 31 August 1964 (goods). The section between Guisborough Junction (Middlesbrough) and Nunthorpe Junction is still used by trains to Whitby via Battersby, where a reversal is necessary. The Codhill branch had a life of only about ten years and in 1874 the land was sold to J. W. Pease for £2,100.

The Pease family lived at nearby Hutton Lowcross Hall but after the collapse of the Pease Bank in 1903 the station provided for their use at Hutton Gate was closed, only to reopen again on 1 January 1904 as a public station. At that time there were very few houses near the station, but now that the station is closed there are houses covering the surrounding fields.

The station at Guisborough, with its train shed covering a single platform, has been demolished since the branch closed. The Middlesbrough & Guisborough Railway had an independent existence of only five years before it was absorbed by the Stockton & Darlington.

In the 1850s the Cleveland Railway was being built southwards from the Tees east of Middlesbrough, towards the ore-bearing Cleveland Hills, and the

Stockton & Darlington looked with strong disapproval on this invasion of its territory. The Cleveland Railway was a protégé of the West Hartlepool Harbour & Railway on the north bank of the Tees and the ore won from the Cleveland Hills was intended for use on the north bank of the river. This meant that the river had to be crossed by a bridge or ferry and the Cleveland and Stockton & Darlington came to blows over this problem after the Stockton & Darlington had placed numerous legal obstacles in the way. The Cleveland Railway was eventually completed, however, and opened from the Tees to Guisborough on 23 November 1861. Within a few years the Stockton & Darlington, the Cleveland, and the West Hartlepool Harbour & Railway were all swallowed up by the North Eastern Railway which, until then, had played only a very small part in the development of Cleveland.

After 1865 the North Eastern had two routes from the Tees to Guisborough – the Middlesbrough & Guisborough of 1854, through Ormesby, Nunthorpe, and Pinchinthorpe, south of the Middlesbrough–Guisborough highway, and the Cleveland Railway via Eston, running north of the main road. However, the two lines crossed just outside Guisborough station and by putting in a link between the two it was possible to close the Cleveland Railway south of Eston. Thus the route from Middlesbrough to Carlin How, Skinningrove (and eventually on to Whitby) was via the Middlesbrough & Guisborough to Guisborough, and via the Cleveland Railway on to Carlin How: the extension was then worked as a Darlington Section (later Central Division) line.

STANHOPE & TYNE RAILWAY

The Stanhope & Tyne Railroad – to give its correct title – was opened in 1834 from quarries near Stanhope, a country market town in Weardale, to the port of South Shields at the mouth of the River Tyne. The company did not obtain an Act of Parliament but built its line on the wayleave principle, commonly used in County Durham and Northumberland, whereby the railway company paid each landowner for the privilege of laying tracks across his land. In most cases the landowner also received a toll based on the amount of traffic passing along the line. However, the amounts demanded for the wayleaves became excessive and the Stanhope & Tyne became insolvent, leading to its dissolution in February 1841.

With the financial collapse of the Stanhope & Tyne Railway, the Derwent Iron Company, with its works at Consett, lost its rail connection and its supply of limestone from the quarries in the hills above Stanhope. To get the line working again, and to obtain a rail outlet to the south, the Iron Company co-operated with a group of Stockton & Darlington directors to build the Weardale Extension Railway between Crook and Waskerley, via Sunniside incline and Tow Law. At Waskerley a connection was made with the Stanhope to Carr House (Consett) line formerly operated by the Stanhope & Tyne, thus providing a through route from Consett to Darlington and the south. The Crook–Waskerley section was opened on 16 May 1845 and this line, together with the Stanhope to Carr House line, became known as the Wear & Derwent Junction Railway.

The line was difficult to work because on the new section it involved climbing the fearsome Sunniside incline, $1\frac{3}{4}$ miles long with gradients between 1 in 32 and 1 in 13, and on the old section the two short but steep inclines necessary to cross the Hownes Gill ravine, as well as the Nanny Mayors incline down from Waskerley. Hownes Gill viaduct was opened on 1 July 1858, striding across the depression on twelve brick arches; a new line avoiding Nanny Mayors incline and the reversal at Waskerley was opened to goods traffic on 23 May 1859 and to passenger traffic on 4 July 1859; and Sunniside incline was finally super- seded when mineral trains began using a new line from 10 April 1867. This meant the easing of the difficulties, and henceforward the line could be worked by locomotives. However, the line remained something of a backwater and it was the haunt of the old double-tender engines of Hackworth and Bouch design.

See Plate 3

William Bouch inspected the former Stanhope & Tyne Railway in October 1844, in readiness for it being taken over by the Stockton & Darlington from 1 January 1845, and he suggested various improvements. To reach the quarries above Stanhope two inclines were used, the first, 1 mile 128 yds long, dropping down from Weatherhill on a gradient of 1 in 13, followed immediately by the Crawley incline, 934 yds long at 1 in 8. The latter section included Hog Hill tunnel. Although this seems to have been built originally to carry only a single track, latterly it did carry two; but because of the limited clearance they were interlaced. The quarries were 795 ft above sea level; Crawley Bank Head was 1,123 ft; and the summit at Weatherhill 1,445 ft: thus the wagons were raised a vertical distance of 650 ft in a travelling distance of $1\frac{3}{4}$ miles.

Both inclines were operated by winding engines because the loaded wagons were travelling uphill, and both remained in use until 1951: traces of the inclines and, in fact, much of the course of the line can be seen from the Consett to Stanhope road.

The ravine at Hownes Gill had been crossed originally by lowering wagons down on a cradle, one at a time, and then taking them up the other side in a similar fashion. Haulage was provided by a winding engine at the foot of the ravine, with a return wheel at the crest on each side. In an attempt to speed up the movement of traffic the wagons were later lowered down one side, and up the other, on their own wheels, three at a time, but as the gradient was as steep as 1 in $2\frac{1}{2}$ the loads in the wagons had to be restricted.

Stockton & Darlington to British Rail

By 1860 the Stockton & Darlington Railway had various points of contact with the North Eastern Railway. That company had been formed in 1854 by the amalgamation of the York & North Midland, York Newcastle & Berwick, and Leeds Northern railways. Its system stretched from Knottingley and Altofts Junc- tion (Normanton) in the south to Berwick in the north, with branches on both sides of the main line, although in fact most of the branches were on the east side, with little penetration to the west. The two main cross-country routes were the Newcastle & Carlisle Railway, opened in sections from 1835 and in 1860 still independent, and the South Durham & Lancashire Union Railway, of which the Barnard Castle to Tebay section was approaching completion under the aegis of the Stockton & Darlington company. At this time the London & North Western Railway was casting speculative eyes on the east-coast ports, which it hoped to reach via either of the two routes mentioned above, and it was imperative for the North Eastern that this intruder from the west be repulsed.

Powers were sought for the amalgamation of the Newcastle & Carlisle with the North Eastern, and the Stockton & Darlington was approached too. The North Eastern connected with the Stockton & Darlington at Eaglescliffe, Darlington, and Bishop Auckland, and with the Lanchester Valley branch under construction from Durham to Consett the North Eastern was infiltrating into the 1825 company's area. Consequently the Stockton & Darlington viewed with favour the approaches from the North Eastern and this attitude successfully stopped the prospects of an invasion from the west, not only via the South Durham & Lancashire Union, but also via the Newcastle & Carlisle, since a feature of the scheme for using that railway was a connecting link from Scotswood to Hownes Gill to give access to the south and east via Stockton & Darlington lines to Tow Law and Bishop Auckland.

However, the Newcastle & Carlisle and North Eastern Amalgamation Bill was rejected, largely because of opposition from the North British. Further attempts were made for a nominally independent link from Newcastle to the South Durham line near West Auckland, although this scheme was largely backed by the London & North Western and the North British, and supported by the West Hartlepool Harbour & Railway, but this was of no avail.

The outcome of all this skirmishing was that the Stockton & Darlington and the North Eastern began working together from 1 January 1861, although not formally amalgamated, and the North Eastern again applied to Parliament for powers to take over the Newcastle & Carlisle. At the same time the Stockton & Darlington sought to absorb the South Durham & Lancashire Union and the Eden Valley Railways. However, the Newcastle & Carlisle amalgamation scheme was withdrawn and the Stockton & Darlington takeover was rejected.

Both schemes again came before Parliament in 1862 and the vital South Durham & Lancashire Union, together with the Eden Valley, both became part of the Stockton & Darlington under the Act of 30 June 1862. The Newcastle & Carlisle Bill was also passed after heavy opposition had been placated, and the amalgamation with the North Eastern was authorised on 17 July 1862. Finally came the formal amalgamation of the Stockton & Darlington and the North Eastern, and this Act received the Royal Assent on 13 July 1863. Thus after a life of 42 years, for 38 of which it had been operating trains, the Stockton & Darlington ceased to exist as a separate entity.

The events of 1863, however, made little difference to the Stockton & Darlington, for a condition of the amalgamation was that the line should be operated by a Committee consisting mainly of former Stockton & Darlington directors but including two from the North Eastern. In addition, three Stockton & Darlington members of the Committee took their seats on the North Eastern board.

The Committee was allowed almost complete autonomy within its own area and its duties were laid down in some 20 sections of the Amalgamation Act, one of which stipulated that any proposed schemes costing more than £5,000 should be first referred to the North Eastern board for approval. Although expected to last for a period of 10 years, the Darlington Committee remained in being until 1876 and its demise appears to have been brought about by the death of William Bouch, one of the remaining stalwarts of early Stockton & Darlington days. He had continued to build, both at Darlington Works and by outside contractors, See Plate 7 locomotives to his own design, remaining faithful to the long-boilered o–6–o type for freight and mineral traffic, whereas the North Eastern's locomotive superintendent, Edward Fletcher, had almost abandoned this type of engine and was turning out in large numbers six-coupled engines with the firebox between the second and third axles.

Even after the abolition of the Darlington Committee, however, the former Stockton & Darlington lines were administered separately in some respects and known as the Central Division of the North Eastern. Certain types of wagons and vans could be seen lettered CD, and the design of signals and signalboxes differed from that on the Northern and Southern Divisions. The Cleveland Railway, absorbed by the North Eastern in 1865, was treated as an extension of the Darlington Section, as was the later extension from Loftus, down the coast to Whitby, and distinctive Central Division features such as signals and signalboxes could therefore be seen from Whitby in the south-east to Consett in the north-west.

And what is there left today of the Stockton & Darlington Railway? Fortunately trains still run over parts of the line opened in 1825, and by using trains between Darlington and Bishop Auckland and Darlington and Saltburn it is possible to travel over some of it.

A Bishop Auckland train from Darlington (Bank Top) station uses for the first mile (as far as Albert Hill Junction) what was originally the Stockton & Darlington's Croft Branch, opened in 1829. This section was sold to the Great North of England Railway in 1838 to form part of its line from Darlington to York. At Albert Hill Junction the original line opened on 27 September 1825 is joined, passing through North Road station (dating from 1842) and Heighington to Shildon. Immediately prior to entering Shildon station the original line branches off to the left, at one time reaching as far as the original terminus at Witton Park, but now serving only the wagon works established on the site of the original Shildon Locomotive Works, where Timothy Hackworth and his men struggled to keep the early steam locomotives in working order.

The section on through Shildon station and Shildon Tunnel to South Church was opened on 19 April 1842 as part of the Bishop Auckland & Weardale Railway, and the final section from South Church to Bishop Auckland on 8 November 1843. Companies associated with the Stockton & Darlington continued far beyond Bishop Auckland to Stanhope and Consett, but now the passenger service terminates at Bishop Auckland, although there is a freight service to Eastgate (in Weardale) to serve a cement works. From 1857, when the North Eastern reached there from Leamside and Durham, Bishop Auckland station was administered by a Joint Committee consisting of North Eastern and Stockton & Darlington representatives, until the amalgamation of the two companies in 1863. It was once the centre of a railway network, with passenger services to Darlington, Barnard Castle, Wearhead, Consett, and Ferryhill. Now all that remains is the pay-train service to and from Darlington.

To the east of Darlington, services from Bank Top station to Newcastle and Saltburn use the 1825 Stockton & Darlington line for part of their journey. For the first four miles from Darlington, however, the journey is over a line opened in 1887, built to enable trains on the former Stockton & Darlington section to use Bank Top station as well as North Road station, and the 1825 route is joined at Oak Tree Junction. The original route westwards from this point, closed to regular passenger services in 1887 when the new route was opened, passed through Fighting Cocks, thence on the north side of Darlington, across the East Coast main line at S & D crossing, to join the Darlington–Bishop Auckland line at Albert Hill Junction.

See Plate 1

Proceeding eastwards, it was at Goosepool, one mile beyond Oak Tree Junction, that the grandstand was erected for the guests of the London & North Eastern Railway to view the memorable procession of old and new locomotives held on 2 July 1925 to commemorate the opening of the Stockton & Darlington Railway 100 years previously. On this stretch the highway from Darlington to Yarm runs alongside the railway on the north side, whilst on the south side of the line is Teesside Airport, with the modern aircraft demonstrating the distance that transport has developed since that historic opening day when George Stephenson drove the world's first steam-worked public railway train.

See Plate 40

Approaching Eaglescliffe the modern trains take a different route from the original, for here the Stockton & Darlington line was moved in 1853 from the south-east side of the highway (now A19T) to the opposite side to facilitate interchange of traffic with the Leeds Northern line opened the previous year. The 1825 route is rejoined by Saltburn-bound trains for a short distance near Bowesfield Junction, but whereas the modern service continues across the River Tees to Thornaby and Middlesbrough, the original trains turned north-eastwards to terminate at Stockton Wharf.

The disused portions of the Stockton & Darlington can be explored at numerous locations. Beyond Shildon, Brusselton and Etherley inclines can be reached easily by road, and parts can be traversed on foot: however, for the 1975 anniversary celebrations it is planned to have most of this section cleared and signposted for walkers. At Shildon itself both Daniel Adamson's coach house and Timothy Hackworth's cottage can be seen, and nearby is a building used by Hackworth as a pattern store, and later by the Stockton & Darlington as a locomotive paint shop. At Darlington, North Road station, opened in 1842, is to be preserved and it is hoped that the two old locomotives, *Locomotion* (built 1825) and *Derwent* (built 1845), now at Bank Top station, will be transferred to North Road.

East of Darlington, Fighting Cocks station, closed in 1887, is still in existence and can be seen from the level crossing: however, this is not the original station. The original course of the line through Preston Park (near Eaglescliffe), abandoned in 1853, appears as shallow earthworks. At St John's Crossing (Stockton) there is a small railway museum housed in the building which is reputed to be "the first ticket office in the world", and it was here that the first rails were formally laid on 23 May 1822, although construction of the line had started ten days earlier.

Stockton & Darlington cottages survive at various sites, usually with a ceramic tile let into one wall: this tile carries a letter and one or two figures, the letter denoting the area, and the figure(s) the number allocated to the property. Stone sleeper blocks can be found at other places, sometimes in their original position, sometimes out of place, and at others built into walls. Various small Stockton & Darlington items – rails, chairs, signals, etc. are to be found in the Railway Museum at York, and a few coaches and wagons have survived. The most impressive relic of Stockton & Darlington interest, however, is the locomotive No. 1275. This was actually built in 1874 after the Stockton & Darlington had been taken over by the North Eastern, but William Bouch was still in charge of the locomotive stock and No. 1275 is of his well-known long-boilered type, with all the axles in front of the firebox. It remained in service until 1923 and took part in the 1925 centenary procession.

The staff of the Stockton & Darlington Railway appear to have been very loth to destroy old documents and records, and when the British Transport Historical Records Department was set up in the 1950s an exceptionally large amount of Stockton & Darlington Railway material found its way to the York office. Even such trivial items as a receipted bill for a night's lodgings for Joseph Pease, away from Darlington on the Company's business, were not destroyed, but the selective thinning-out of such material has still left a most valuable collection of Stockton & Darlington material, now in the care of the Public Record Office in London. Darlington Library also has a collection of letters from George Stephenson and others connected with the Stockton & Darlington Railway.

Photographically the Stockton & Darlington Railway is not well represented. That well-known early railway photographer, R. E. Bleasdale, visited Shildon in the 1860s, when he photographed some of the early locomotives out of use and awaiting cutting up for scrap, but he does not seem to have pointed his camera at any mineral or passenger trains, even stationary. Thus photographs of Stockton & Darlington rolling stock – both passenger and goods – are extremely rare. Fortunately some working drawings of such vehicles have survived.

As might be expected, it was the mineral traffic which developed so spectacularly on the Stockton & Darlington. The amount of coal and coke carried in the first nine months of operation amounted to 42,983 tons. For the full year of

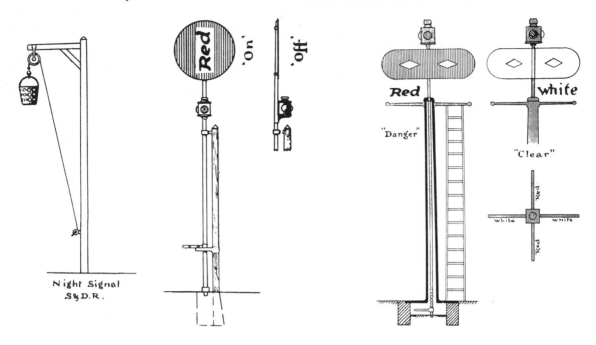

2   Signals used on the Stockton & Darlington Railway. On the left is a version of the common "disc" type, the disc turning sideways on to the driver to indicate "all clear". The other type, on the right, was patented by William Bouch, the Company's Engineer.

1860 it had risen to 2,045,596 tons, and ten years later it had more than doubled and reached 4,341,631 tons. Similarly, general merchandise traffic increased from 4,407 tons in the first nine months (to 30 June 1826) to 587,765 tons in the year ending 31 December 1860.

By 1860 the company required 15,058 wagons to carry its traffic, but of these only 400 were of 9-ton or 10-ton capacity: all the others were chaldron wagons, so long favoured by the mineral-carrying lines in north-eastern England, largely because of the limited loading facilities at the mines, and unloading facilities at the docks and staiths.

Coaching stock amounted to 136 vehicles in 1863: 15 first-class coaches, 40 second-class, 45 third-class, and 36 composites; together with 20 horse boxes, 16 carriage trucks, and 26 luggage and parcels vans.

When it opened in 1825 the Stockton & Darlington possessed one locomotive, but at the end of its existence in 1863 it had 157: 27 for passenger trains; 127 for mineral and goods trains; and 3 old engines out of use – *Locomotion*, *Sunbeam*, and *Manchester*.

The first dividend paid by the Stockton & Darlington amounted to $2\frac{1}{2}\%$ for the year 1826. By 1831 it had risen to 5%; by 1835 to 6%, and in 1836 it reached double figures at 11%. The maximum dividend was reached in the years 1839, 1840, and 1841, when the rate was 15%, but after that it gradually declined, reverting to single figures – 7% in 1849 – although it reached 10% again in 1857. However, it had fallen to $7\frac{3}{4}\%$ by 1863, the year of amalgamation with the North Eastern Railway. The North Eastern dividend for 1863 was $4\frac{3}{4}\%$!

Over the same period, 1826–63, the total receipts increased from £9,194 to £494,690, with the coal traffic alone amounting to almost 90% of the total in the early days and falling to around 70% by the time of the amalgamation.

In County Durham and Northumberland coal had for many years been transported in wagons running on wooden rails, either drawn by horses or utilising gravity down the slopes leading to the River Tyne or the coast. The development of the locomotive, giving great haulage power, and the iron rail, with its reduced friction, led to the haulage of greater loads at a higher speed, thus reducing the cost of the coal at the point of shipment.

This change brought about the building of numerous steam-worked lines in the north-east, the main object of which was to carry coal for profit, with the passengers only a necessary evil. Most of these new lines were public railways, following in the steps of the Stockton & Darlington and carrying coal from any colliery adjacent to the line, although the original concept of the coal owner carrying his coal in his own wagons on his own line persists to this day in the shape of the National Coal Board.

The introduction of improved means of transport led to the rapid expansion of industry in the north-east, particularly in the heavy industries such as the manufacture of iron and steel, and shipbuilding. The railway could carry the coal and limestone cheaply and quickly to the blast furnaces, particularly in the Middlesbrough area, where the nearby Eston Hills provided a supply of ironstone. The resulting iron could then be used to build ships on the Tees, leading to the development of other industries necessary to engine and fit out the ships.

Much of the coal mined in the north-east was carried in these ships to the south of England, or across the North Sea, and coal loading ports existed all the way up the coast from Middlesbrough to Amble, but it is a far cry from the 42,000 tons carried by the Stockton & Darlington to Stockton in the first year of the railway, to the 6 million tons of coal shipped at Blyth alone in 1961.

They were men of foresight who put up the money for the Stockton & Darlington Railway, built the line, and operated it.

1 "S. & D. Crossing" was for many years a landmark on the East Coast main line, just north of Darlington station, where the original Stockton & Darlington line crossed it on the level. This part of the Stockton & Darlington has now disappeared, and with it the signal box.

2 Heighington, a station built by the Stockton & Darlington and continuing in use, little changed, under the LNER.

3   Constructing the Hownes Gill viaduct, 1857–8. It was built of brick, 730 ft. long, with a maximum height of 150 ft. The Stanhope & Tyne Railway had used an extraordinary contraption for lowering wagons, one by one, down one side of the ravine and up the other, at inclines of 1 in 2½–3. This viaduct, which replaced it, was built by the Stockton & Darlington Company.

4   Belah viaduct on the South Durham & Lancashire Union line (cf. p. 30). It was designed by (Sir) Thomas Bouch, was just over 1,000 ft. long and 196 ft. high at the maximum. It cost £32,000. It continued in use until the line was closed in 1962.

5 *Locomotion*, as it was formally mounted outside North Road station, Darlington.

6 *Derwent*, built for the Stockton & Darlington Company by W. & A. Kitching of Darlington in 1845. This engine is also preserved at Darlington.

7   Bouch's six-coupled goods engine of the "long-boiler" type, with all the axles in front of the firebox. The pipe behind the chimney was part of a mechanism for heating the water. These engines were built from 1866 to 1874.

8   4–4–0 locomotive of a class built in 1872–4 to Bouch's designs and nicknamed "Ginx's Babies". It is seen here at Saltburn, whence it worked one express service daily to and from Leeds in 1875–8. These engines were also used on the steep line from Darlington through Barnard Castle to Tebay.

9   Shildon Works, with one of Bouch's 0–6–0 engines.

10   The celebration of the Jubilee of the Stockton & Darlington Railway: unveiling of the statue to Joseph Pease in the Market Place, Darlington, 27 Sept. 1875.

2 The Railway in Britain 1825-1947

The lessons taught by the Stockton & Darlington Railway were studied elsewhere in the United Kingdom, and far beyond. It was visited and reported on by engineers and public men from all over Europe – from France and Germany and Bohemia – and repeatedly by Americans. They saw for the first time a mechanical public railway as a working concern, and though the social and economic conditions under which it was built might differ widely from those that were familiar to them, the example it set could be applied wherever the potential traffic seemed to justify it. The performance of the steam engines, crude and imperfect though they were, made an indelible impression. As a shrewd American engineer put it: "There is no reason to expect any material improvement in the breed of horses in the future, while, in my judgment, the man is not living who knows what the breed of locomotives is to place at command."

The railway was studied above all in Britain. In 1824–6 the stock market was in the grip of speculation, some of which was concerned with railways and stimulated by the Company's achievement. The fever passed in 1826, but it did not discredit the projection of well-founded plans. In 1824–8 nine railway companies were authorised by Parliament, to employ mechanical haulage, wholly or in part, from their inception. They totalled 110 miles in length: four each in England and Scotland, one in Wales. The projectors of such lines as these – and many more were projected than built – made their way steadily to observe the new railway in use, and to see its locomotives at work.

Of these nine companies, one proved to be outstanding: the Liverpool & Manchester. It was a much bigger enterprise than any that had preceded it, and when it was opened to public traffic on 17 September 1830 it differed from the Stockton & Darlington in three important respects. It was worked entirely by mechanical power: by locomotives except at the Liverpool end, where stationary steam engines were employed to haul the trains up the steep incline at Edge Hill. It concentrated primarily on passenger traffic (goods were not conveyed regularly until December 1830); and it showed for the first time what the railway could do in that way on a large scale, carrying 460,000 in the first year of its working, more than four times the number that had been conveyed by the horse-drawn coaches between Liverpool and Manchester in the past. Finally, all the traffic on the railway, in passengers and goods, was handled by the Company itself. The See p. 24 Stockton & Darlington had licensed private contractors to operate the modest passenger service it afforded. The Liverpool & Manchester Company kept direct control from the outset of every vehicle that moved on its system.

The new railway became at once a national institution. Substantial lines were soon brought into use elsewhere. Across the Atlantic a similar mechanically-operated railway was opened at Charleston, South Carolina, before the end of 1830; in France there was one between Lyon and St Etienne in 1832. But the Liverpool & Manchester retained its primacy. Connecting two of the great commercial cities of Europe, it demonstrated more completely than any other

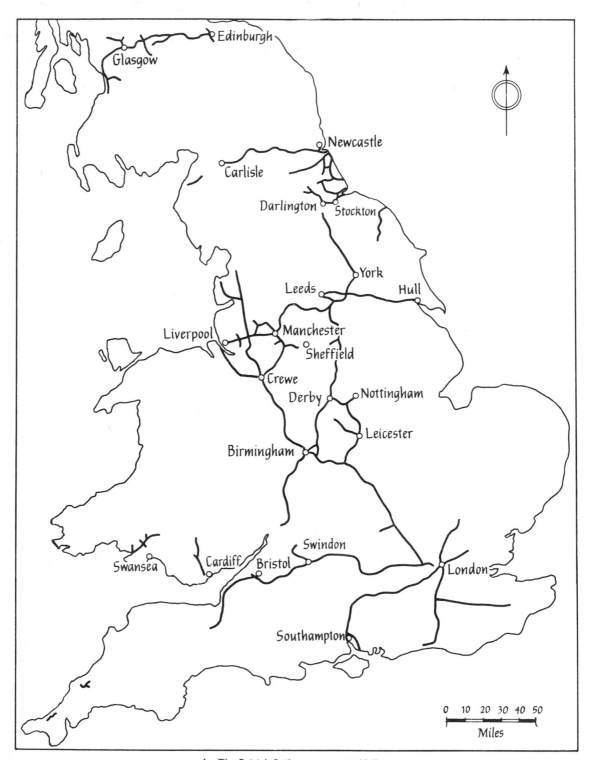

1   The British Railway system in 1842

railway the full potential that the new means of transport could offer for the future. A contemporary writer hailed it truly as "the Grand British Experimental Railway".

Still, it was only some 30 miles long. The next step was to apply this successful experience to a railway running over a much greater distance, a main trunk route. That idea had already been canvassed in 1824–5, when plans were brought forward for railways, for example from London to Brighton and Birmingham, not to mention what then appeared such fantasies as lines to Wales and Scotland. Some of these projects were now revived, and in 1832–5 companies were established to build railways over three such routes, radiating from London: to Southampton, to Bristol, to Birmingham and so northward to link up with the Liverpool & Manchester line in Lancashire. These railways were not constructed all at once. Great difficulties were encountered in their making – new difficulties that had not arisen on the Stockton & Darlington or the Liverpool & Manchester; but by 1842, when all these lines were completed, together with some important extensions and feeders, the country had a railway system nearly 2,000 miles in length. The railways earned some £4 million in that year, of which 70% came from passenger traffic, 30% from goods.

In Britain – as, with a few exceptions, in North America – the work was all in the hands of private companies; 50 of these contributed to the total that has just been given. On the Continent of Europe, however, many of the railways were built at the direction, or at least partly under the control, of the State. In Belgium, for example, a railway system was carefully planned by the Government to serve political as well as economic ends. The British Government did no more than impose certain restrictions on the promoters of railways, to safeguard the interests of property and to ensure public safety. For railways were dangerous things. The locomotive was a machine with great reserves of power, which might explode or take its train into a collision. Men working on the line were always exposed to injury or death. Hence the meticulous codes of rules the railways adopted – often, in early days, under the direction of stiff ex-military or naval men: H. P. Bruyères, for instance, of the London & Birmingham (later London & North Western) Company, of whom a friendly junior officer said that he was "noted as a disciplinarian, with a well-drilled staff, trained to obey, but not allowed any liberty as to suggestions for improvements". Even at the outset the railways began to establish their own *esprit de corps*, railwaymen to become a distinct element in the society of Britain as a whole.

The railways of this country were very expensive. The cost of land was usually high, sometimes extortionate; the political process of promotion involved heavy legal costs; engineers and surveyors were scarce, and at a premium. Much money was wasted on things that could, with time and greater experience, have been achieved more economically, or on mistakes that could have been avoided altogether. But time, above all, was lacking. Once the railways caught on, everyone became eager to join in their extension. Towns were afraid of being left off the system; manufacturers wanted to see their goods distributed faster and more

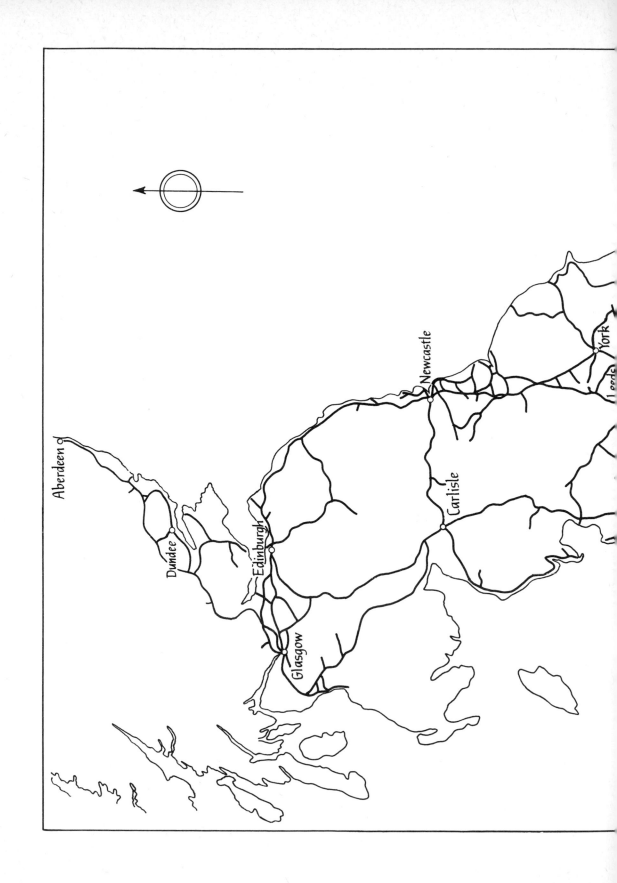

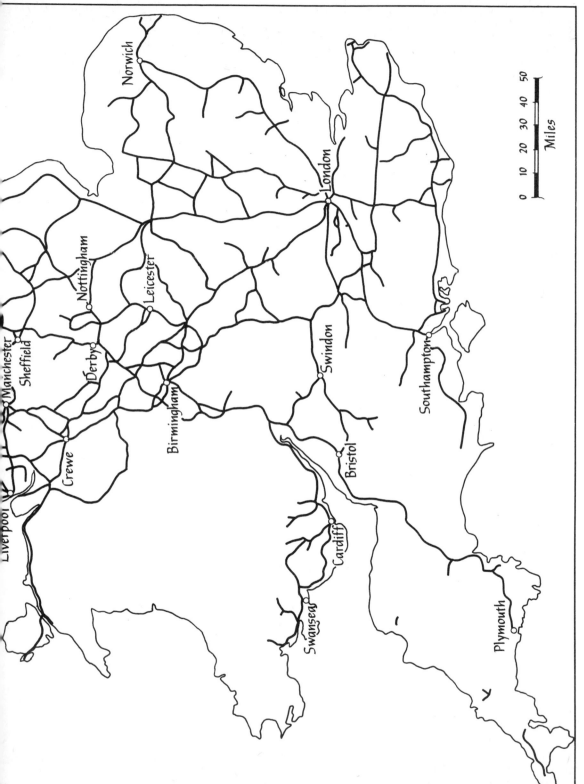

2 The British Railway system in 1852

cheaply; farmers began to realise the revolution the railway might bring in their markets; the landowners who had opposed them at first came to appreciate the benefits they offered, and to welcome them. Scores of thousands of individual men and women throughout the United Kingdom saw the chance to get rich quick opening up ahead. In 1824–6 railway projects had not played the central part in the general speculation; but they had been conspicuous enough for the fever to be called "railway mania". The same phrase was used, more justly, for a second outbreak in 1836–7. The third, in 1844–7, has always been the Railway Mania; rightly, for it was on a far bigger scale, and railways were the chief element in it.

No figures can fully convey the size and nature of this frenzy. In January 1846 the Prime Minister, Peel, stated cautiously that plans for 815 new railways had been legally lodged before Parliament, at a prospective cost of £350 million – or well over six times the entire expenditure of the nation in that year. These projects envisaged the building of nearly 21,000 miles of railway. In the end, during the whole of this great Mania, about 8,600 miles were authorised. Some of these lines were constructed slowly, others not at all.

Looking back over the accounts of the madness, one can see no limits to what might have resulted from it. Any number of absurdities stand out among the projects of these years. Of those that actually came before Parliament, consider the London & Dublin Approximation Railway (through Bicester and Llangollen: capital £6 million) and the four companies all named the Great Welsh Railway. These projects did exist. Punch had a fine time conceiving others that did not, but were only a little more ludicrous: the Eel Pie Island Railway, the Gretna Green Direct Atmospheric. Countless small investors, who had been lured into the business guilelessly, were ruined. Truly the development of railways in Britain was a wasteful and hazardous business.

Yet it must be fairly judged. If the process was disorderly, it did produce results. The British railway system grew faster, the railways themselves were in many respects more efficient than those on the Continent. In 1849 Britain had three times as much railway open as France, ten times as much as Belgium, and more than the whole of the rest of Europe put together.

By 1852 the British railway system extended from London to Aberdeen (by two routes, through Glasgow and through Edinburgh); to Hull, Yarmouth, and Dover; to Plymouth; to Gloucester and Swansea; to Holyhead. Great cross-country routes had been established also: from Bristol through Birmingham to York, from Liverpool to Hull.

Yet the system had grave defects. There were then some 75 independent companies operating railways in the United Kingdom. The facilities for interchange between them, for passengers and goods, were far from complete. The instrument for organising them had been there for ten years past: the Railway Clearing House, which had been established in order to settle the financial arrangements between the companies, dividing among them the money received for services they rendered jointly. If a passenger bought a ticket, for example, from Leicester to Norwich, the sum he paid would have to be apportioned between the Midland and the Eastern Counties Railways, which carried him. That was the function of the Railway Clearing House, and a very useful one it was in mitigating the troubles that arose from allowing the railways to be owned by a host of separate companies. But by no means all the companies were members of the Clearing House. Not until 1865 could it be said to include every one that was of major importance. Companies were not obliged to join it; and whether they belonged or not, they were free to provide, or to refuse, through bookings as they pleased.

In the Midlands and the South the lines were laid to two different gauges. The 4 ft 8½ in. gauge prevailed over most of the country; but in Scotland many of the early railways preferred the gauge of 4 ft 3 in., and the Great Western Railway and some adjoining companies had adopted the much broader gauge of 7 ft. By 1852 the 7 ft gauge had come to extend over the whole South-West of England, South Wales, and as far north as Wolverhampton. Where the two gauges met, as at Gloucester and Salisbury, passengers had to change carriages, and goods to be trans-shipped. The evil could be reduced by the laying of a third rail, to produce a "mixed gauge"; but this was an unsatisfactory expedient that entailed technical complications, for example in the working of points and crossings.

A serious effort was made by the Government in 1845 to end the nuisance of the two gauges, through the appointment of a Commission to investigate the problem. But by the time it reported, in February 1846, there were about 275 miles of broad-gauge line in operation, out of a total of 2,225 miles for Great Britain as a whole, and it seemed impracticable to require the conversion of the broad gauge to the narrow in order to produce a uniform system. It would have been exceedingly expensive; it also seemed foolish, since in some important respects the broad gauge was able to show a superiority, in actual working, over the narrow. The Government therefore confined itself to limiting the spread of the broad gauge northwards and eastwards. It had, moreover, profited from the lessons taught by the two gauges to establish a third, of 5 ft 3 in., as the standard for Ireland.

No important difficulty of this sort arose on the Continent, except at international boundaries, with Spain and the Russian Empire, which used wider gauges than the normal 4 ft 8½ in. Within each state, the Government was usually able to impose a single gauge, and to compel the few dissidents to abandon their practices. In the United States, however, a multitude of gauges abounded, with serious results for the economic life of the country until they were made uniform, after the Civil War, in the 1870s and 1880s.

Construction and Working

How were the railways built, and the trains worked, in these early days?

See Plates I and II In their civil engineering much experience was derived from the roads and

bridges of the eighteenth century; even more from the canals, which had achieved some great feats of tunnelling. The railways had to solve many new problems, however, arising from the track itself, the "rail way" in its bed, its laying (should it rest on stone blocks or wooden sleepers?), and the composition of the rails. They needed entirely new kinds of equipment. Look at Robert Stephenson's Round House at Camden Town (still in use today, though for a purpose remote from railways). No stable for horses had ever been like this. But then horses could turn themselves round, whereas locomotives could not: hence the turn-table on which the whole building pivoted.

Railway stations too had to be designed in large measure from first principles. The ordinary simple goods station, with a platform, a wooden shed, and a crane, could be taken over from the canals; but very soon much more complicated structures were required. The wayside passenger station was often at first little

3 The London & Southampton Railway under construction at Weybridge. This was among the early contracts of Thomas Brassey, undertaken in 1837–8.

4 The North Midland Railway at Bull's Bridge, Derbyshire. The Cromford Canal passes over it; the road has been relegated to a small bridge on the right.

5 Entrance to the Engine Shed at Camden Town, London & Birmingham Railway. Lithograph by John Bourne, showing his usual meticulous attention to detail. The chimney on the right served the stationary engine that hauled the trains up the incline from Euston.

6   Goods station at King's Cross, Great Northern Railway (1852). Built above the Regent's Canal, it provided for the interchange of traffic between railway, road, and water.

more than a wooden hut on a very low platform, but as traffic developed this simple unit had to become more elaborate, with booking and parcels offices, waiting rooms, and a house for the stationmaster. As for the terminal stations in big towns, they soon grew to an unprecedented size. Their roofing and glazing presented new problems; so did the access to them from the crowded streets (much more crowded than we often realise) of Victorian London or Manchester. The most splendid of these early stations in Britain are Paddington in London and the Central station in Newcastle, extended today but not altered in essentials. A number of others survive, wholly or in part, from the Early Victorian age: Newark (Castle), for instance, Kettering (distinguished for its elegant ironwork), **See Plate 16** Abergavenny; accomplished works of architecture at Huddersfield and Stoke-on-Trent.

The trains that ran into these stations look to us tiny by comparison with those we are accustomed to now. But they ought not to be thought of in that way. The right comparison to make is with the stage-coaches, their predecessors. A coach held 4 passengers inside, 8 or at the most 12 on the roof: so it was a unit for the conveyance of not more than 16 people. By the 1850s even a minor train would usually offer places for 80, a major one for 200 or more; and none of those would be conveyed on the roof. The conditions in which passengers were carried varied greatly according to class, and from company to company. The first-class carriage was a version – usually a good deal superior – of the inside of the old stage-coach. The second-class was much less roomy and more spartan; but still, in most states of the English climate, preferable to the coach's roof. The stage-coaches had provided for no third class. That was one of the railways' great innovations. After the passing of Gladstone's Act of 1844, passengers enjoyed certain minimum rights, which put them far ahead of those who had travelled most cheaply by coach. Those who were conveyed by "Parliamentary trains" were to be protected from the weather in their carriages; the trains had to run each weekday and serve every station, at a speed of not less than 12 m.p.h. (faster than the fastest coach), for a fare of a penny a mile, which was less than any coach had charged. The companies varied considerably in their treatment of Parliamentary and third-class passengers. This kind of travel was far from comfortable. Neither was it cheap: the penny was still a valuable coin to working men. Still, if a really poor person was obliged to make a journey he could now do so at an unprecedented speed, and with a convenience inconceivable to the previous generation, for whom it would have been possible only on foot.

Many railway companies disliked the passengers travelling at these cheap fares. But all were compelled to carry them; and they came to contribute a rapidly-

7 Newcastle Central station, opened by Queen Victoria and the Prince Consort on 29 May 1850. It was designed by the Newcastle architect John Dobson and remains one of the grandest early railway buildings in Britain.

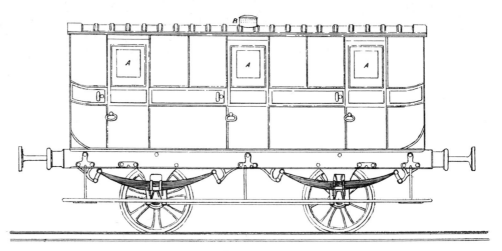

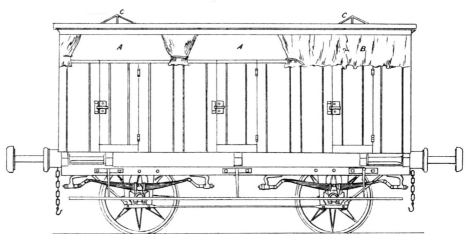

8, 9 Carriages used for conveying "Parliamentary" passengers, 1845. The upper one, of the Midland Railway, has glazed windows in the doors; in the lower, of the London & South Western, the open space marked "A" could be closed in bad weather by curtains.

increasing proportion of the railways' revenue. In 1850 they accounted for nearly 30% of the total; by 1860 the receipts from the third class exceeded those from either of the other two.

The locomotives that hauled these trains quickly developed a long way beyond *Locomotion* and *Rocket*, though by a steady process of evolution, not through one great improvement like that which had been marked by the blast-pipe and the multi-tubular boiler. Those two engines had both been carried on four wheels. In the course of the next 20 years it came to be accepted that it was better to mount the machine on six. This conclusion was not reached without much noisy argument. The question was carefully investigated in 1841, when it transpired that already nearly three-quarters of the engines in use on the principal lines were six-wheeled. They were thought to be steadier – they probably were. But Robert Stephenson rested his preference for six-wheeled locomotives on a

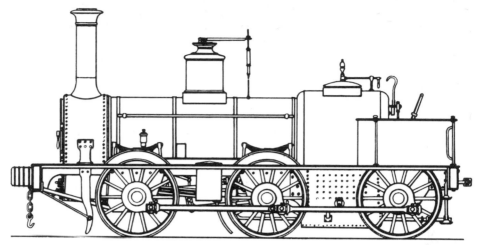

10 Locomotive built for the Leeds & Thirsk Railway in 1848 by Kitson Thompson & Hewitson of Leeds. The original British standard goods engine.

different ground: that they allowed a larger boiler to be provided without increasing the load on the axles, and so on the track, which often proved brittle under the weight imposed on it.

Before the forties were out, two further developments along the same lines had taken place. The eight-wheeled locomotive had established itself securely on one railway, with Daniel Gooch's engines of the *Great Western* and *Iron Duke* class — easily the largest, at the time when they appeared, to run anywhere in the world.

See Plate 11

Thirty of them were turned out between 1846 and 1855, and they (together with another small batch, built later) worked the chief express trains on the broad-gauge Great Western line until the broad gauge itself came to an end in

See Plates 12 and 13

1892.

These splendid machines were not, however, typical of British railway practice. At almost the same time the six-wheeled engine came to take on a new form. This was the goods engine with six coupled wheels, inside cylinders and frames, and the third axle placed behind the firebox. The first of this kind began to appear in 1848, almost simultaneously from manufacturers in Leeds and Bolton. The Leeds engines may be taken as the prototype of many thousands that followed. They were used by every major railway in Great Britain, except the Great North of Scotland and some of those running under special conditions in London and South Wales. Over 900 of them came out, to one design, on the London & North Western Railway; over 700, much later and more powerful machines but still bearing the same characteristics, were built by the Midland and London Midland & Scottish companies. It might indeed be said that the type endured for a whole century: for the last o–6–o engine of this kind was turned out from Swindon Works after the railways had been nationalised, in 1948. That is not a mere laughable illustration of British conservatism. The engines were, of course, enlarged and improved in many ways as time went on. But they showed exactly the qualities permanently needed for working the traffic in this country. Strong, steady, simple, cheap to build and run, they were the truest representatives of British locomotive practice.

That practice was followed with close attention elsewhere in the world. In the 1830s Britain, having pioneered the development of locomotives, supplied them to every customer as fast as manufacturing resources would allow. The first locomotives to run in, for example, Italy and Russia and Argentina were all made in Britain. Robert Stephenson & Co. in Newcastle were active in the export business; so were Sharp Roberts, and later Beyer Peacock, of Manchester. As railways grew all over the world they encountered here and there special problems of their own, and British locomotive builders were often called on to help in solving them. Robert Stephenson's were asked, for example, to supply machines suitable for working the line between Turin and Genoa, with its exceptionally steep gradients, in 1855. Their solution took the form of double locomotives, placed back to back so that they could be controlled by one crew. That idea had originated three years earlier in Belgium. It came to have a quite unforeseeable future in a somewhat different form.

The Festiniog Railway had been working in North Wales, for the carriage of slate, since 1836. For economy it had been laid out to a very narrow gauge – a fraction under 2 ft. It was operated by gravity and horse-power until 1863, when locomotives were introduced. The first of these proving insufficient to deal with heavy trains, in 1869 a double-ended machine was tried, designed by R. F. Fairlie, and it was an instant success. Fairlie (a noisy publicist) went on to proclaim the advantages of narrow-gauge railways in general, operated by his engines. Visitors came to look at his handiwork, anxious to see if it could be applied in Hungary and Scandinavia and Russia. They found it could; and during the rest of the nineteenth century the narrow-gauge railway established itself as an agent in developing countries where the standard gauge would not have been economic, in Central and South America, in India and New Zealand. Large versions of the Fairlie locomotive were still being built in Glasgow for the Mexican Railways in 1911. The world owes a debt to this little railway – which remains happily working today; much the most historic of all "preserved" lines – in the far north-western corner of Wales.

Expansion and Competition

The British railway system was, as we have seen, an untidy one in its origins and early growth. The Government resolutely declined to go beyond acting as a regulator and a protector of the public. So here the railways of the nineteenth century never made up a planned system, as the Belgian and the French railways did; they were promoted by private enterprise, almost unfettered. In the mid-Victorian age the system grew more untidy still through the force of competition, which produced a duplication of routes. By 1880, among the fifteen largest towns in Britain all but three (Bristol, Hull, and Newcastle) had competitive routes to London to choose from. From Manchester, Glasgow, and Edinburgh there were three routes, on all of which express trains ran, in hot rivalry with one another. Contrast the situation in France, where not one of the great cities — except, in a very restricted sense, Bordeaux — ever enjoyed competitive services from Paris.

There were advantages here and drawbacks. The British railways have always provided a much more frequent service of trains than those on the Continent; and at least until 1914 it could be said that, judged by any reasonable test, they were on the whole faster. That is attributable in part to the density of the population of Britain, and to the rapid growth in the size of its towns; but also to the force of competition. Once this standard had been set, it lasted, even when the power of the competitive principle was reduced. And although goods rates usually had to be kept in step, manufacturers and traders also enjoyed some benefits from competition. Nevertheless, competition did not necessarily produce better service. Portsmouth was served by two railways, which were rivals only for the wooden spoon. Conversely, some towns that were served by one railway alone were satisfied with it. The Corporation of Ipswich thought in 1880 that its train service, provided solely by the Great Eastern Company, "now leaves hardly anything to be desired".

One thing was perfectly clear, both to the critics and to the supporters of competition. The practice was expensive: for it led to the duplication of routes, at enormous cost. Kent provides an outstanding example. Until 1858 it lived under the monopoly of the South Eastern Railway. Then came the East Kent, whose title was soon glorified into "London Chatham & Dover"; and the two companies came to furnish competing services to every town of consequence in the county except Folkestone. Sometimes the competition was useful: from Canterbury and Dover two routes were established to London, serving different intermediate tracts of country. Much more often, however, it was ludicrous, resulting in the provision of double sets of trains, stations, staff, and equipment, as well as many miles of additional railway, often traversing empty agricultural land. It all meant large capital expenditure on services that could not possibly pay. The high initial cost of railways in this country thus rose much higher still. They suffered, to a greater degree perhaps than the railways of any other country, from the burden of over-capitalisation, and in the end that weakened them gravely.

By 1880 the system was complete, for the whole island of Great Britain, in outline. In the past 20 years it had been extended widely through Wales, northern England, and Scotland; across to Aberystwyth, north and south from Bangor to Carmarthen; over the wild Pennine country from Skipton to Carlisle and from the original Stockton & Darlington line westwards to Cumberland; from Carlisle to Hawick and Edinburgh; north-westwards to Oban and Strome Ferry; to the far north at Wick and Thurso.

This did not bring the railways to the peak of their development, however. In 1914 the system comprised just over 20,000 miles of line in Great Britain. Nearly a quarter of that had been constructed since 1880. A process of infilling had continued, by the building of branch lines, often serving remote agricultural communities and very small towns indeed – Westerham and Abbotsbury in southern England, for example, Strathpeffer, Dornoch, and Lybster in the north of Scotland. The force of competition, too, still drove the building of new railways forward. That could be useful or frivolous or tragic. Both the last adjectives might be used of the most ambitious of all the competing lines of these years, the London Extension of the Great Central, which was opened in 1899. The idea on which its promotion rested – that additional facilities were urgently required between Sheffield, Nottingham, Leicester, and London – was specious. It was a splendid white elephant; a noble manifestation of late Victorian engineering, and an economic disaster.

But not all competitive lines were so futile. Some of those in South Wales, for example, had a logic, even a necessity of their own. The Barry Docks & Railway Company arose in response to the needs of the Rhondda, which could not get its coal shipped without intolerable delays at Cardiff. Unlike the Great Central, which never managed to pay its Ordinary shareholders a penny, the Barry was financially very successful – in terms of dividends, the most successful railway company ever to operate in Great Britain. Even at the end of its life in 1913–21 it was paying 9–10% every year on its Ordinary shares.

The other ambitious new company launched in these years, the Hull & Barnsley, enjoyed a success midway between these two. It was, just as evidently, a child of competition: the work of citizens of Hull, where there had long been dissatisfaction with the services afforded by the monopolist North Eastern Company. Its construction proved far more difficult than had been expected. The railway, excluding the dock with which it was associated, cost £4 million; its 53 miles, opened in 1885, had taken five years to complete, from the passing of its Act; at the beginning of 1887 the Company was bankrupt, and it remained insolvent for nearly three years. It held on, nevertheless, and by 1896 it was able to pay a dividend on its Ordinary stock, which rose to $4\frac{1}{2}$% in the last years of its independent life. But it achieved this modest prosperity only when it had succeeded in reaching a measure of agreement with the North Eastern. Competition could not maintain it alone.

The new construction in these years also included two other sorts of railway. Some important lines were built to improve the existing system, shortening distances or easing gradients. The Great Western did most in this way, with its new main lines from London to South Wales (1903), to the West Country through Westbury and Castle Cary (1906), and to Birmingham (1910), as well as the Birmingham–Bristol line through Stratford-upon-Avon (1908). These were often spoken of as mere "cut-offs"; but they had an aggregate length of 145 miles.

The other important group of new railways were urban and suburban. In 1863 London had provided itself with the first underground railway in the world: the Metropolitan, running from Paddington to Farringdon Street. This was slowly extended to make an Inner Circle, completed in 1885. It was a shallow line, built in cuttings and tunnels close to the surface of the ground. Its construction

See Plates 14 and 15

therefore involved much disturbance of streets and of the increasingly complicated system of services, of sewers and gas-mains, that lay underneath them, as well as danger to the foundations of houses. Presently an alternative sort of underground railway began to be advocated: one at a deep level, enclosed throughout in a tunnel, a "tube". Such a railway had already been built in 1870: the Tower Subway, under the Thames. But it quickly failed as a railway, and the tunnel was turned over to pedestrians. The first successful railway of the kind was the City & South London, which was opened from a station near the Monument to Stockwell in 1890. Though this line too experienced grave teething troubles, it has an importance second only to that of the Metropolitan: for it was the first electrically-operated tube railway anywhere. It was followed eight years later by a second, from Waterloo to the Bank, and afterwards by a whole group of lines, opened in 1900–14. The system then stood virtually complete, apart from extensions out into the suburbs, until the 1960s.

See Plate 28
See p. 189

London rejected entirely the elevated railway, adopted so widely in New York and other American cities, and to a small extent in Paris. It put its faith in the deep-level tube, and the example it set has been studied and imitated all over the world.

Glasgow was the only other city in Britain to build a tube railway: a circle line, opened in 1896 and operated by cable traction until 1935, when it turned over to electricity. Liverpool had two urban railways of its own. The Mersey Railway dived at a steep gradient under the river; it was operated by steam locomotives, in conditions of ferocious discomfort, from 1886 to 1903, when electricity displaced them. The Overhead Railway – Britain's unique "elevated", on the American plan – began work in 1893; it was the first railway of that kind to be electrically operated.

Elsewhere the new railways built near the centre of cities were piecemeal extensions of the existing system. Sometimes they fulfilled a dual purpose, by providing a new main line as well as a service for the suburbs: like the Birmingham West Suburban Railway, opened in 1876 and adapted to this purpose nine years later. When built entirely for suburban traffic they often proved expensive liabilities: the Nottingham Suburban Railway of 1889 (partly financed by the Borough Council) is a case in point. For at this moment the railway was facing a new kind of competition: from tramways, which had first appeared in the sixties, began to be mechanised (with steam or cable traction) in the eighties, and triumphed when they turned to electricity on a large scale near the close of the century. They were formidable rivals to the railway: convenient in that they ran along roads and did not pick up only at fixed stations wide apart, cheap (they were often supplied with their power from municipally-owned electricity works), and clean. The railways' suburban traffic seemed to melt away before them.

In Scotland the Glasgow & South Western Company capitulated to the trams in 1902, withdrawing its service between Govan and Springburn and concentrating its attention almost entirely on the traffic to the outer suburbs of Glasgow and to the Ayrshire coast. That was one policy: inglorious but clear-cut, realistic, and

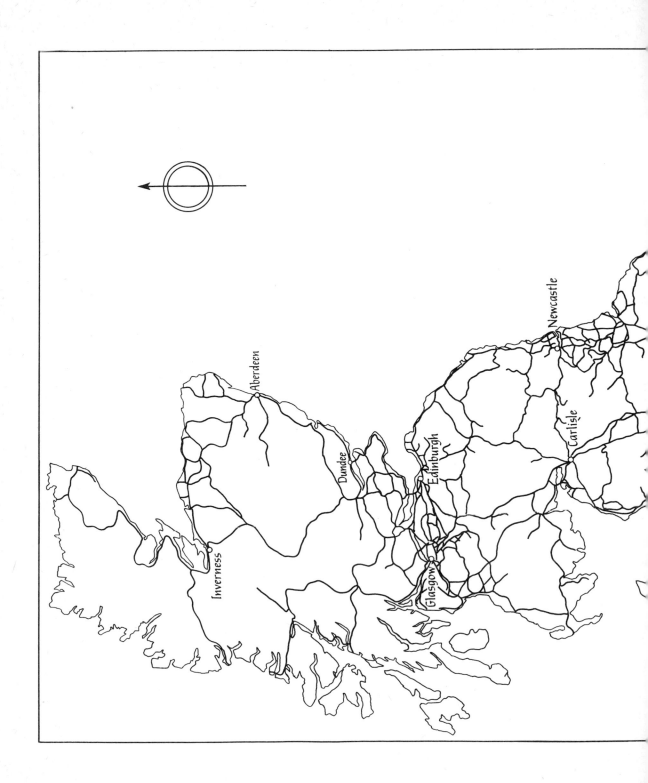

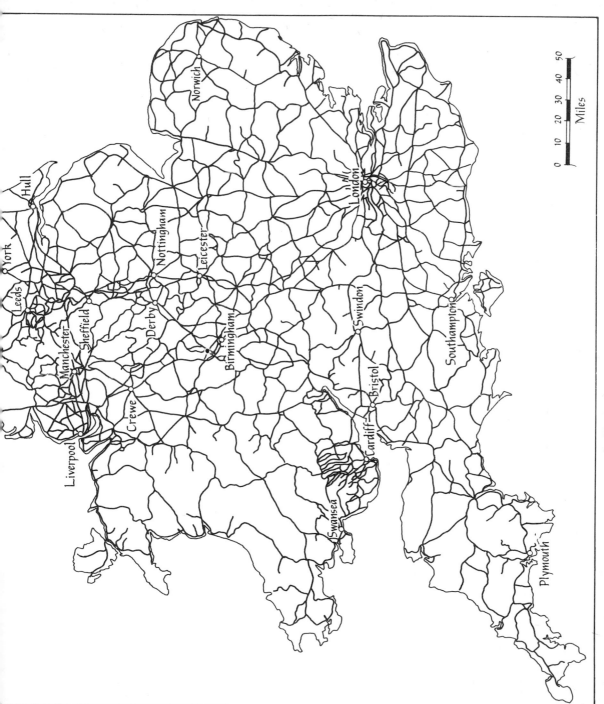

3   The British Railway system in 1914

probably the best from the shareholders' point of view. Close-packed suburban trains were never easy to operate. On some lines, such as the Great Northern into London, they were a major obstruction to the free flow of the railway's other traffic and forced it to undertake very expensive new engineering works, like providing additional tunnels. The business was hardly remunerative, for season-ticket holders were carried at extremely low rates. The Great Northern often expressed the wish that it could rid itself of the "suburban incubus".

See Plate 26

Those railways that turned to fight the trams were successful only in part. They tried a variety of expedients. They could electrify their own lines, as they did on Tyneside, in Liverpool and Manchester, and in London; and sometimes this proved the remedy. On the South London line, for example, the London Brighton & South Coast Company watched the number of passengers fall from 8 million in 1903 to 3 million five years later. The line was electrified late in 1909; by 1910 there were 8 million passengers travelling on it again. The Brighton Company went on to consider plans for the electrification of its entire system. They were maturing by 1914, when the outbreak of war ended them. By that time two other companies were engaged on the same work, the London & South Western and the London & North Western. Their first electric services were introduced in 1915–17.

Some railwaymen believed that the challenge of the trams could be met without incurring the cost of electrification. The Great Eastern, which operated an exceptionally dense suburban traffic out of Liverpool Street, made a spirited and not unsuccessful attempt to demonstrate that it could provide a steam-hauled service comparable with an electric one. James Holden, its Locomotive Engineer, built a ten-wheeled engine, *Decapod*, which on test in 1903 developed a speed of acceleration and a tractive effort as great as could be attained by an electric locomotive. But this sprightly mammoth was kept out of regular service because its weight was too much for the bridges on which it had to run; and strengthening them was held to be prohibitively expensive.

See Plate 27

Other railways turned to the "steam railcar": a combination of passenger carriage and steam locomotive, operating a shuttle service without needing to be turned round, stopping at frequent halts, which were intended to emulate the trams by bringing the service to the passenger. A number of the larger railways adopted this expedient for a time. On most lines the cars had only a short vogue, at its height in 1903–8. They were underpowered and they were inflexible units, which could not meet any sudden demand for additional accommodation; and with their steam engines built-in they were apt to be unpleasantly hot. Some railways thought highly of them all the same. In 1901 the Deputy-Chairman of the North Staffordshire Railway, in despondency, told the shareholders that it was "almost impossible to compete with the electric tramway". Four years later the Company introduced steam railcars through the Potteries with great success, and by 1910 it had recovered most of the lost traffic. The Great Western, which was one of the first railways to adopt them, made more use of them than any other. Whereas most companies never had more than a dozen, it built 100. It used them for suburban traffic, but also to serve groups of small settlements lying close together, as in the Stroud valley in Gloucestershire, and on rural branch lines.

The battle with the electric tramways was only one sign that the railways were losing the preponderance they had enjoyed in the country's transport system. They were challenged too by the internal combustion engine, by the motor-bus and the road lorry, in the opening years of the twentieth century. At first they met the new rival successfully, by going into the business themselves. From 1903 onwards many railway companies began to operate motor-bus services, as feeders to their own lines; a few, like the Lancashire & Yorkshire and the North Eastern, also owned and ran motor goods lorries. What is curious, looking back today, is to see how irresolute the railways were in this matter. The Great Eastern, for example, built in its works at Stratford a fleet of motor-buses, used all over East Anglia. It sold them off, and so helped to lay the foundation of the Eastern National Bus Company, which later became its most dangerous competitor. Again the Great Western showed the stiffest determination, retaining its motor-buses and developing their use, though still not far enough to master the threat when it came in the 1920s.

Economic and Social Effects

What effects did the building of all these railways have upon the economy and society of Britain? The question is obvious, but difficult to answer with real precision.

Many people have made assertions on this matter, bold and insufficiently considered. They frequently remark, for instance, that the population of a town grew larger in the years following the arrival of a railway, and that the railway caused that growth. The statement may be true; occasionally it can be proved. The Great Northern Company removed its locomotive works from Boston to Doncaster in 1853. The new establishment brought 949 men into the town, together with 1,562 women and children; so that there, at a stroke, a railway increased the population by some 25%. The case is seldom so clear-cut. Much more often this kind of statement is mere unfounded guesswork. Railways did not necessarily stimulate any significant increase of population. Reading got its first one in 1840, and the firms of Huntley & Palmer and Sutton's, the seed merchants, were set up there at once, partly on account of that new facility: yet the population of the town increased over the next ten years more slowly than in any other decade of the nineteenth century. Where country towns were concerned, it is clear that the railway might do nothing, over the years, to augment the population; that might even fall. Moreton-in-the-Marsh was placed on a main line in 1853; but fewer people lived there in 1901 than when it had arrived. Walter Bagehot (who was born and died in Langport, a very small country town) explained this confidently: "Every railway takes trade from the little town to the big town because it enables the customer to buy in the big town." But his crisp generalisation is not a formula, valid everywhere.

See Plate 24

See Plate 25

Some things we can say positively. The railway did create a few industrial towns, or make them out of market towns and villages: like Crewe and Swindon and Ashford, like Caerphilly in Wales and Inverurie in Scotland. Railway manufactures made a substantial contribution to the industrial development of a number of towns. The locomotive builders of Manchester and Glasgow have been mentioned; large wagon works were established at Gloucester and Birmingham. Much later, the manufacture of signalling and brake equipment came to be centred at Chippenham: the 60% increase in the population of the town in 1901–11 must be attributed very largely to the removal there of the English division of the Westinghouse business.

The lack of adequate railway facilities was a standing grievance with some towns, and loudly voiced. Sheffield and Nottingham both complained that they had been left off the main lines of railway communication between London and the North, and that their trade suffered in consequence. The deficiency was rectified in due course. Sheffield was placed on a main line in 1870, Nottingham ten years later. What difference did that in fact make to them? Nobody so far has told us. Perhaps nobody can.

And what about those towns that never got a railway at all? By the beginning of the twentieth century the largest towns in England and Wales more than three miles from a station were Wedmore (population 2,700) and Ambleside. One county town, Beaumaris, was in the same position; and one cathedral city, St David's. Three other towns with a population around 2,000 also lacked a railway: Shaftesbury, Mere, and Clun. None of these places had had a thriving industry, which was removed or killed owing to this deficiency; at the beginning of the railway age Shaftesbury was making only shirt buttons, and that on a diminishing scale. Ambleside, alone among them, would probably have benefited from the building of a railway, which was foiled by the defenders of the Lake District; but its physical situation would always have prevented any substantial growth.

As for villages, the railway companies' records contain many petitions asking for stations to be built. Cases were sometimes investigated with great care. When the decision was adverse, and the inhabitants determined, the argument might go on for years: as at Bramley, which first asked for a station on the line between Reading and Basingstoke in 1848 and got it at last in 1895.

Railways made their contribution to British agriculture, in a general way during its prosperity from the 1840s to the 1870s and more deliberately in the hard times that followed. They were particularly important in the cattle trade, reducing the losses suffered on the road from droving. The construction of light railways, to standards lower than those normally required, was advocated for country districts. A few such lines were built under the guise of tramways, like the Wisbech & Upwell, which was opened in 1882–3 and for a long time successful. Many more appeared after the passing of the Light Railways Act of 1896, some of them designed almost wholly to assist the farmer: the Selby Wistow & Cawood, for example, and the Mid-Suffolk.

One other illustration of what the railway did for rural England – something that no other form of transport could have undertaken then: it founded the traffic in early vegetables and flowers from Cornwall. By the late eighties, at the height of the season, 60 truck-loads of broccoli and more were being dispatched from Penzance in a day, and 3,000 boxes of narcissus from Scilly might go up by the night mail, to appear at Covent Garden next morning.

The total activity of railway companies ranged far beyond the conveyance on their own tracks of the traffic that offered. They developed important ancillary services, which had wide ramifications through British society. Their business extended on to the water. They absorbed many canals, strangling some as trouble-some competitors but carefully fostering others, like the Shropshire Union. They operated steamships, on their own account or through contractors, across the North Sea, in the English Channel, and to Ireland; not only the famous and imposing ferries from Dover and Holyhead, but tiny ventures all round the coast, now forgotten – services from Aberdovey to Waterford, from Cardiff to Burnham, from Shoreham to Jersey. Three Scottish railway companies raced their steamers against one another all over the estuary of the Clyde. The railways owned a chain of important docks, from Grangemouth to Southampton. They played a leading part in the development of the Victorian hotel. Each of the chief companies except the London & South Western had one at its London terminus. There was an hotel that was worked, or at least owned, by a railway in every one of the largest British towns except Leicester. In Scotland the railways invested profitably in golfing hotels, like that at Turnberry created by the Glasgow & South Western.

See Plate 30

The railways interested themselves directly in a large number of industries too. The Great Western owned collieries. The London & North Western had a quarry at Shap, the London & South Western one at Meldon, to provide them with the ballast they needed for their permanent way. Their works proliferated subordinate industries. Leather, soap, and bricks were made for the railway at Crewe; as early as the 1850s the Eastern Counties Railway had its own printing works at Stratford. Their fingers were in pies everywhere throughout Great Britain.

What then, finally, did they contribute, as they grew, to the nation at large? It is only lately that economic historians have begun to consider that complex question in detail. Some Americans have suggested that the part played by rail-ways in the economic development of the United States in the nineteenth century has been over-estimated; that many of the changes they brought about could have been achieved by other means, particularly through water transport. In this country the conditions were somewhat different. A similar extended investigation of the British railways in the years 1840–70, by Dr G. R. Hawke, comes to the conclusion that the part they played here was considerably greater in proportion; that railways "could not have been sacrificed in 1865 without the need to com-pensate for a loss of the order of 10% of the national income". That is an answer to the first part of the question posed at the start of this section: an answer in economic terms, much the most carefully considered that has yet been given, though not a final one – no answer to it will ever be final. The human and social effects of railway building are harder still to analyse. As we look back at the Victorian world we are only now starting to appreciate and assess them.

Declining Popularity

The railways' position began to deteriorate towards the end of the nineteenth century. They were under political attack. In some fields, though not in all, they exercised a monopoly. Traders complained that their rates were too high, and inequitable between commodities and districts. Exhaustive Parliamentary inquests were held into their pricing policies. These revealed many practices that were anomalous, and some that were indefensible, as well as many others that were reasonable but misunderstood. Altogether, they brought the railways into disrepute – more disrepute than they deserved. At the same time they were under attack for their neglect, real or supposed, of safety precautions. When accidents occurred, Government Inspectors probed into their causes. From 1871 onwards they were also liable to involve public inquiries. The reports of all these investigations were published. They provoked alarm that was often justified: above all because they revealed how many accidents were due to the conditions in which railway servants were employed. The men were sometimes obliged to work very long hours; they carried – notably signalmen and engine-drivers – great responsibility; the equipment in their hands was not always of the best. Gradually a feeling grew up that the railway companies were mean and harsh employers, exploiting their servants and disregarding the safety of their passengers. As a generalisation it was unjust. Much could be said on the other side. In many respects the railways were good to work for, and recognised by their servants as such. But in a society in which working-class opinion was becoming increasingly powerful, in itself and in its influence over middle-class politicians, these criticisms did railway managements much harm. They were the background to the growth of trade unionism, which they helped to foster.

Railwaymen had been by no means pioneers in this development. They had formed a friendly society, which may have had some of the character of a trade union, as early as 1839, and a strike on the London & North Western in 1848 provided evidence of combination: representatives of four other companies attended the strikers' meetings. In the sixties two unions appeared in succession, representing the footplate men. They looked imposing, and the second of them organised a successful strike on the Brighton line in 1867. But when it tried conclusions with the North Eastern seven weeks later it collapsed. The way was then open for a general union: the Amalgamated Society of Railway Servants of 1871. That body soldiered on. Its difficulties did not lie exclusively with the employers; they were almost as great with the men themselves. Within ten years the footplate men were busy organising their own separate union once more. No wonder the General Secretary of the Society questioned what the word "Amalgamated" in its title might mean. The drivers and firemen considered themselves a caste apart. The Amalgamated Society of Locomotive Engineers and

Firemen (ASLEF) emerged as a consequence in 1880. The Society of Railway Servants eventually came together with some smaller unions to form the National Union of Railwaymen (NUR) in 1913.

Railwaymen as a whole came to form a sizable component of the society of Great Britain. A detailed analysis was made of them in 1873, showing that 260,000 were employed by the railways in England, Scotland, and Wales: that is, a trifle under 1% of the whole population. This total was broken down as follows:

Administration (Departments of Secretary, General Manager, Storekeeper, and Accountant; police)	3%
Traffic Department (e.g. station staff, guards, porters, shunters, signalmen)	39%
Locomotive Department	30%
Engineer's Department	21%
Miscellaneous (including men employed in telegraph and steamship business)	7%
	100%

Besides those employed by the companies, a large number more worked in businesses that were dependent on or connected with the railways. In other words, taking families into account, in the mid-Victorian age railway employment supported over 4% of the entire population. The railways' prosperity therefore concerned not only capitalists and small shareholders but the labour force of the country as a whole. The very nature of the employment helped to cushion that labour force against adversity. Most railwaymen occupied posts that had of necessity to be filled. In a year of bad trade a shopkeeper could dismiss any of his assistants; mill hands could always be laid off, or put on short time. The same could not be done with railway staff. If a train was to run it must have a driver, a fireman, and a guard; goods traffic could not be handled at all without clerks and carters, porters and warehousemen; safety devices had to be applied by an irreducible minimum of signalmen. Unprofitable train services were scarcely ever abandoned. Only an insignificant number of minor lines were closed to passengers in the mid-Victorian age: the Winsford branch, the lines from Towcester to Stratford-upon-Avon and from Orton to Rothes in Morayshire are among the few – and the first two of those were subsequently reopened. Even when the Hull & Barnsley Company was in Chancery, its trains still ran. In a world in which employment fluctuated alarmingly the railways offered – they were compelled to offer – a degree of security to be found in very few other services. So the companies and their servants were bound together by a mutual dependence; and in ordinary conditions, whatever mild grumbling might be heard, that kept labour relations good-tempered.

The companies too did a good deal, by the standards of the age, to care for their employees. Medical funds were established for railwaymen as far back as the 1840s, even by some very small companies, like the Preston & Wyre. Surgeons were retained – the Great Western gave its man a house at Swindon rent-free on condition that he attended its servants without charging them; and the Company built a small hospital for its men there in 1872. Many railways helped to support benefit and friendly societies. The Brighton Company established a savings bank for its employees in 1852; by 1870 six others had done the same. The London & South Western showed a particular solicitude for children orphaned by the death of men in its service, by helping to support a private institution in Lambeth, which eventually grew into a full-scale orphanage, still active, at Woking.

All gestures of this kind were paternalistic; and as the century went on some railwaymen declared their dislike of them, for that reason. There were many cases of hardship that the companies ignored, and many others that, to our way of thinking, they treated with stinginess or a want of sympathy. It has always to be remembered, however, that the officers and directors were answerable to the shareholders. Those shareholders were not a consciously-organised body of harsh employers; but very many of them depended on the income earned by their shares, and naturally objected to anything they thought undesirable charity at their expense.

It is fairer perhaps to criticise the railways as employers on a different ground. They unquestionably overworked a good many of their servants, and this became an increasing cause of grievance. In 1861 a deputation of engine-drivers asked the Government, in vain, for a statutory limitation of hours of work. The companies often observed that hours had to be kept flexible to allow for the fluctuating demands of traffic, and that was a proper contention; but excessively long hours were often demanded as a regular condition of employment. This was most striking where footplate men and signalmen were concerned; but it did not apply to them alone – in 1866 a stationmaster at Whitehaven, for example, worked for $13\frac{1}{2}$ hours on three days in the week, and from $15\frac{1}{2}$ to $18\frac{1}{2}$ on the rest.

In the 1860s and 1870s the public became alarmed at the frequency of railway accidents. They were two dreadful decades in this respect, beginning with the Tottenham accident on the Eastern Counties Railway and ending with the fall of the Tay Bridge. Even those who had no particular sympathy with labour as such became alarmed at the implications of overwork for their own safety. Gradually the matter became a politicians' cry. In 1885 Lord Rosebery described it as a public scandal; six years later a Parliamentary Committee was set up to investigate the problem. The Inspectors considered that six or seven of the accidents they reported on every year were attributable, wholly or in part, to excessive hours of work. Appreciating the need for flexibility, the Committee shrank from recommending that the State should impose a fixed working day; but it indicated means by which the Government might persuade the companies to remedy the evil. The railways were embarrassed by the odium they incurred from this cause; and that, reinforcing pressure from the State, helped to bring about a general improvement in working conditions.

This improvement came under another compulsion, too, gradual for a time but then peremptory: the demands of the trade unions, which grew steadily in the eighties and nineties. At the opening of the new century they were able to threaten one company after another with a showdown. That generally remained a threat, no more, but not empty. When they put it into effect they did not always succeed. On the Taff Vale Railway in 1900, confronted with a tough General Manager, they failed, at a cost that was alarming. But the unions' political influence was now strong enough to bring about a change in the law (arising out of that railway conflict) in 1906, which favoured them. Next year they threatened to call a national railway strike; four years later they put the threat into effect. The strike of 1911 lasted only a few days and did not extend to all companies alike; nor did it secure every demand the unions put forward. Nevertheless it set a grim precedent, remembered by the companies – and by the nation, still dependent as it was, overwhelmingly, on its railway system.

The railways were indeed no longer as popular, as clearly symbols of progress, as they had been when they were new. Politicians attacked them from both sides of Parliament. There was unending complaint about their rates and about the services they provided. That was disagreeable enough for the railways; but it was made far worse by their deteriorating economic state. The costs of running them rose steadily. In the sixties working expenses had represented some 48% of the companies' total receipts; in the next decade that figure rose 5% higher; in the opening years of the twentieth century it had climbed to 63%.

These mounting costs were incurred in several ways. One was the expense of improved safety devices: continuous brakes, communication between passengers and train crew, the interlocking of points and signals. Many railway managers had resisted these changes. They often did so largely on account of the expenditure involved. But that consideration could not be acknowledged in public as paramount. The plea they most usually put forward was that with increased mechanisation railwaymen would become less vigilant themselves, more inclined to rely on the machine. It is a familiar type of contention, and not wholly false.

The managers often advanced another argument too, which was better founded: that the new devices urged on them were imperfect, or that more than one was available, and therefore they should take time to choose, from experience, between them. That was quite true of passenger communication, the need for which became luridly apparent in the light of the Müller murder on the North London Railway in 1864. In this matter the Board of Trade was caught out, satisfying itself with one system and endeavouring to make it compulsory in 1868 and then, in the face of its manifest failure, withdrawing approval from it five years later. No really effective system came into use until the 1890s. As for continuous brakes, there was a multitude of systems available. To be effective the brake had to be not only continuous throughout the train but also automatic in its application; and only two types fulfilled that requirement satisfactorily – the automatic vacuum brake and the air brake invented by the American George Westinghouse. The Government was rightly concerned that the railways

NOVELTY IN GLASS.

BELINDA, ABOUT TO ARRANGE HER BONNET AT WHAT SHE SUPPOSES TO BE THE NEW LOOKING-GLASSES ("AND A VERY GRACEFUL AND CONSIDERATE IDEA, TOO, ON THE PART OF THE RAILWAY!"), SPEEDILY DISCOVERS HER MISTAKE, AS SHE IS CONFRONTED BY THE FACE OF AN IMPERTINENT YOUNG MAN IN THE NEXT COMPARTMENT.

11 The murder of Thomas Briggs by Franz Müller on the North London Railway in 1864 aroused great agitation among railway travellers because the victim might have been saved if he had been able to summon help when attacked. Some companies pierced the wall between compartments with circular apertures to enable passengers to see what was going on next door. These became known as "Müller's lights". Here is *Punch*'s view of a possible consequence.

should adopt the improved brake in some form as quickly as possible, and made it compulsory as a result of the fearful accident at Armagh in 1889. But it shrank from specifying which pattern should be used: with the result that the railways in Britain divided, a majority choosing the vacuum whilst the Westinghouse was preferred by the remainder. Through trains running over lines that adopted different systems had therefore to be equipped with both: every express from Euston to Glasgow, for instance, the London & North Western Company having fixed on the vacuum brake, the Caledonian on the Westinghouse. Like so much else in the history of British railways, it was an untidy business.

Signalling systems were now becoming much more elaborate, again under steady pressure from the Board of Trade, which for many years published an annual return from the companies of the progress they were making with the interlocking of points and signals. By the 1890s this patience had been rewarded. Only one notable laggard remained: the Great North of Scotland Railway. Its pertinacity in wrongdoing triumphed: when the inquiries were discontinued as superfluous, since interlocking was almost universal except on a few remote and

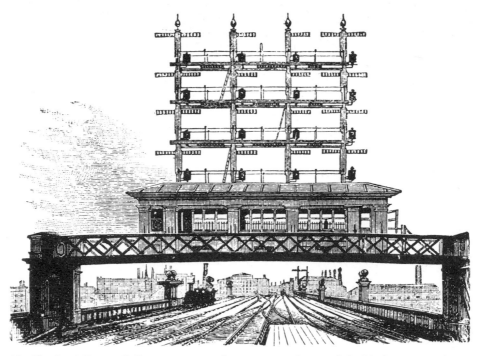

12   The South Eastern Railway was among the pioneers in the use of the block system and
in the interlocking of points and signals. This installation at Cannon Street (by the firm of
Saxby & Farmer) went into use when the station was opened in 1866. It was a cause of great
confusion at first, before the men had had time to "learn the frame".

poor lines, it still reported that the number of its installations interlocked was
less than 90%.

Other safety devices improved in these years, sometimes in direct response to
accidents. Two very bad collisions occurred, for example, on single lines at
Thorpe, near Norwich, in 1874, and at Radstock two years later. In 1878 Edward
Tyer patented the electric tablet instrument, which governed admission to each
section of a single line; and this, gradually improved in detail, provided efficiently for the working of single lines in safety and, where it was necessary, at a
good speed. The Great Western made important experiments with a device to
give an audible warning to the driver whenever he passed a distant signal at
danger. This was tried out on the Henley and Fairford branches in 1906 and
installed on the main line between Paddington and Reading in 1908–10: the
forerunner of a complete system of automatic train control. Automatic signalling
also appeared in Britain in these years. It was first employed here, on an open
line not in a tunnel, on the Liverpool Overhead Railway in 1893. The first
illuminated track diagram anywhere in the world was installed in 1905 in the
signal-box at what is now called Acton Town station, on the District Railway
in London.

Rolling-Stock and Locomotives

All these improvements were expensive; but they were not the only additional costs that the railway companies and their harassed managers had to bear in these years. In many respects they steadily improved their standards of service. Though this may have brought them more business, it also involved heavy new expense.

The improvement dates from the 1870s, and it began by affecting the man in the third class, not in the first. Hitherto on most British railways – as almost everywhere in Europe – he had been kept out of express trains. In 1872 the Midland Company stated that in future all its trains, fast and slow alike, would include third-class carriages. The other companies, which had not been consulted, expressed indignation, but most of those north of the Thames soon fell into line. (The companies in the south-east of England and the Great Western, competing with the Midland very little, did not.) Then in 1874 the Midland abolished second class altogether, lowering its fares at the same time; and finally in the following year it set about upgrading its third-class carriages. Previously their seats had been of bare wood. Now the Midland promised to upholster them all forthwith. Again there was consternation – some of it among the shareholders of the Midland itself. Only a minority of other companies dispensed with second class, though a substantial number more did so in 1893 and nearly all the rest in 1911–12. But all those who competed with the Midland – and it was in many respects the most highly competitive line in the country, with a system that came to extend from London to Swansea and Carlisle – had to consider offering their third-class passengers the same standard of comfort. Here is a clear gain, accruing from the competitive principle. No Continental railway did anything like this in the nineteenth century.

So the Midland Company courted the poorer traveller. But it did not pay attention to him alone. At the same time, in 1874, it introduced Pullman cars to Britain from the United States: "parlor cars" for day travel and cars with beds for use at night. Both were very much on the American model. The day carriage was open from end to end. Most Englishmen continued to prefer the compartment (as many of their grandchildren do still), and the day cars did not prove a great success, though they established themselves happily enough on the Brighton line from 1875 onwards. Nor were the arrangements in the sleeping cars altogether liked.

They were not quite the first sleeping cars to run in Britain. The North British Company had introduced one to work between Glasgow and London in April 1873, whereupon its West Coast rivals followed suit six months later. The American vehicles were superior to the British in two most important respects. They were heated by steam and they ran on eight wheels, on a pair of bogies, whereas the North British and West Coast sleepers were mounted on six wheels, which always gave a jolting ride. The Midland set about at the same time building its own ordinary carriages for long-distance trains with bogies. Together with the

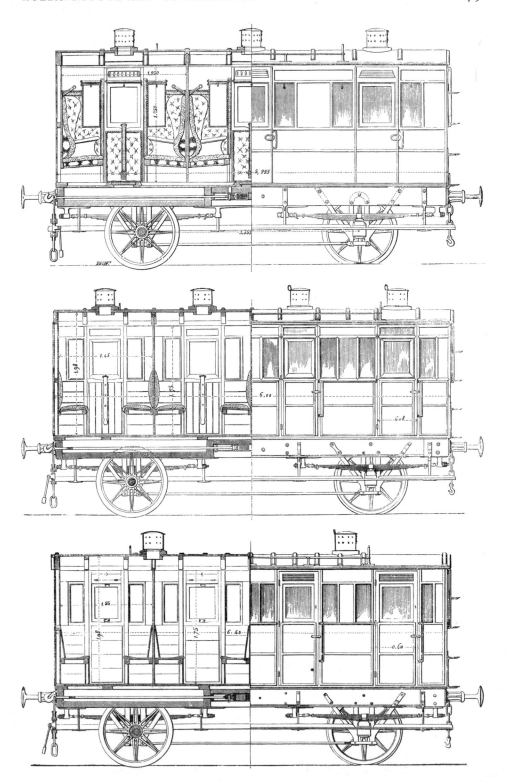

13, 14, 15 Great Northern Railway carriages, 1st, 2nd, and 3rd class, c. 1860.

16   The railway refreshment room was a frequent target for Victorian satire. Here is Richard Doyle's lively sketch of the one at Swindon in 1849, among his "Manners and Customs of the English".

other improvements that have been mentioned, they helped to attract patronage to the competitive service it started to run between England and Scotland in 1876.

Finally, in this remarkable decade came some improved arrangements for the feeding of passengers making long journeys. Up to this time such facilities had been confined to the provision of refreshment rooms, with a special dining stop *en route*, say of 10 or 20 minutes at Swindon or Preston or York. In 1876 the London & North Western Company introduced a service of luncheon baskets, available at Chester to passengers on the Irish Mail. Then a much bigger step forward was taken by the Great Northern Railway, which began to run a dining car between King's Cross and Leeds in 1879.

In the course of the next twenty years all these developments were taken further, and one more was added. The eight-wheeled carriage, mounted on bogies or radial trucks, became common on express trains, though it was far from universal; the Great Northern, for example, continued to cling to the six-

I The best-known timber bridges were those designed by Brunel for the Great Western Railway and its neighbours, but there were many others. This one was on the Great Northern, at Bardney, Lincs. It was designed by (Sir) William Cubitt and completed in 1848.

II Ballochmyle Viaduct, built by the Glasgow, Paisley, Kilmarnock & Ayr (later Glasgow & South Western) Railway, $1\frac{1}{2}$m. south of Mauchline, Ayrshire. It was designed by John Miller and constructed in 1846–8. It is 163 ft. above the water, and with its span of 181 ft. it was, when new, the widest masonry arch in the world.

wheeled pattern, to its passengers' discomfort. The provision of lavatories grew increasingly general at this time, one or a pair serving each carriage, reached by an internal vestibule, until a new sort of gangway appeared joining carriage to carriage – not the open platform (which the American Pullmans had afforded), but the enclosed corridor. This was first seen on the Great Eastern Railway in 1891, on its boat train from Harwich to the north of England. It included a dining car to which the new gangways allowed access, for the first time in England, while the train was travelling. A second corridor train began to run on the Great Western in 1892. Another was put into the afternoon service between Euston and Scotland in 1893. That 2 o'clock train was known on the line for many years after as just "The Corridor".

Now these were expensive innovations, not only in capital cost, but in another way too. They increased the dead weight per passenger that had to be hauled. The introduction of the internal vestibule or corridor meant the loss of a pair of seats in each compartment; dining and sleeping cars were heavy, and the facilities they offered for carrying additional passengers were disproportionately small. The only answer was to provide a pair of locomotives for each train, or one much more powerful than those that had previously sufficed. Again, it was an expensive necessity. Here is one main element in the increase of working costs in the late Victorian age.

For these reasons and others, the locomotive in Britain now took some strides forward. The engines of 1870 had represented in most respects no more than a cautious improvement on those that had run twenty years earlier. The use of steel, which had come in tentatively in the sixties for boilers, tyres, and rails, now increased. In the seventies some important changes of design began to appear, not in goods engines, which continued to be mainly of the six-coupled pattern dating from 1848, but in those intended for passenger service, express and suburban. For express work the type with single driving wheels (exemplified by Patrick Stirling's famous engines on the Great Northern) went out on some lines in favour of the four-coupled engine, which offered greater adhesion, more evenly spread; and smooth running was improved by giving it a leading bogie. This type, the 4–4–0, evolved first in Scotland in 1871–3. Its use then spread gradually to many English companies – the Lancashire & Yorkshire, the Midland, and the London & South Western, for example; though others, like the Great Northern, still for the time rejected it. The same eight wheels, arranged in reverse with the bogie at the back, came to characterise a popular type of late-Victorian tank engine for suburban and branch-line work.

With express engines of this kind, British practice and experience developed in much the same way as they did at the time on the Continent. As for the United States, the 4–4–0 had long been known as the "American" type. In some ways, however, the British did things differently. They generally placed the cylinders of the locomotives inside the frames, when everywhere else it was usual to put them outside. More important, whilst the French and other European railways went in for compound locomotives, using steam simultaneously at high and low pressure,

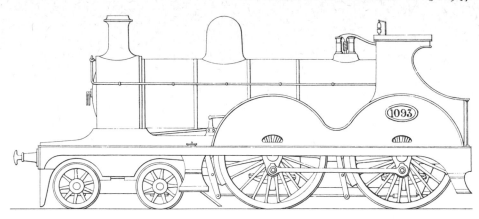

17   The Victorian 4–4–0 express locomotive: a late example of 1891, designed by (Sir) John Aspinall of the Lancashire & Yorkshire Railway. It had exceptionally large driving wheels (7ft. 3 in.): nearly the largest coupled wheels ever placed under a locomotive in this country. There were 40 of these engines, which worked the Company's services all over South Lancashire and across the Pennines from Manchester to Leeds. The last of them was broken up in 1930.

in Britain that system did not catch on. With one great exception: on the London & North Western F. W. Webb adopted it wholeheartedly; hundreds of compound locomotives were turned out to his designs between 1882 and 1903. He considered them more economical; those whose duty it was to make them work in service knew that they were complicated and unreliable. Many other British railways tried the compound locomotive, but all rejected it save the Midland, which developed it, in one design only, from 1901 onwards. Everywhere else the "simple" engine prevailed in this country, though the compound had a long vogue in Ireland.

The simple British express engine was capable of much further development. That came about gradually, on one railway after another, in the eighties; critically – again in Scotland, on the Caledonian – in 1896, when J. G. McIntosh produced his locomotive *Dunalastair*, incorporating a boiler materially larger than any similar machine in this country had carried before. The example thus set was quickly followed elsewhere. It extended even to Belgium, which imported a number of these very machines and developed them, little changed, into a standard pattern of its own. The Belgian railways, after experiments similar to those made in Britain, had likewise rejected compounding.

See Plate 21

Hauled by the simple engine, the British express train continued to set an example to the world. It is pleasant to turn from the shortcomings we have looked at to consider these services. They were much faster than any in Europe, as Foxwell and Farrer showed conclusively, and with engaging humour, in their book *Express Trains English and Foreign* in 1889. Indeed that book was able to begin by an assertion of superiority that at first takes away one's breath. In defining an "express train", the authors apply a different standard to those in Britain from that which they use for Europe. To qualify as an express in Britain (or the United

States) they lay it down that a train must run at 40 m.p.h., including stops; anywhere else it qualifies if it attains 29. This they justify unanswerably by pointing out that if they had adopted the same standard throughout they would "not collect from the whole of Europe as much 'express' mileage as is run by our small Great Northern Company".

But Foxwell and Farrer pointed out something else quite as important as the high speeds of British trains: the much better total service they provided. In Britain the third-class passenger was admitted to 93% of the expresses — as against 59% in Belgium, about 27% in France, South Germany, and Italy. At the other end of the scale of wealth, the charge for a sleeping berth over a comparable distance was between seven and nine times as high in France as in Britain.

In all such matters Britain remained well ahead of her neighbours. Her expertise in railways too continued to stand high. The great manufacturing firms were still See Plate 19 sending locomotives all over the world. But they were under increasingly strong challenge from Germany and the United States. That is neatly summarised today in the beautiful museum of the Netherlands State Railways at Utrecht. There you see four locomotives, trim and British in every detail, one (a replica of the first to run in the country) built in Northumberland in 1839, two from Manchester (1864, 1881), one more from Glasgow (1889). They are balanced by three built in Germany. The dates of those three are symbolic of a great change: 1880, 1914, 1931.

It was beginning to be noted in the nineties that foreign engineers came in smaller numbers to study British railways; the traffic seemed now to be more in the opposite direction. The British had evolved the kinds of accommodation and equipment they required for their particular traffic; but that traffic was in many ways peculiar to the island. The goods wagon provides an example: the British open-sided truck, to take 7–10 tons of coal or merchandise. To Americans, and to many Europeans, it was an absurdly small unit. Would not covered box-cars, and wagons of much greater capacity, be more economic? They found them so; and in terms of simple statistics that was true. British railway managements were not entirely deaf. A few big coal wagons, mounted on bogies, were put into service. The Great Western tried one in 1888, the Caledonian built a batch in 1903. But they were not a success, for two reasons. The consignments to be conveyed were generally small, and it was difficult to secure full loads except for coal. But for coal traffic these big wagons were useless on most of the private colliery lines owing to their sharp curves. So the old wagons continued in use See Plate 31 everywhere, though wood began to give place to steel in their construction early in the twentieth century.

Here again we see the great part played by private industry in determining the policy and character of the British railways. Tens of thousands of private See Plate 32 owners' wagons ran on them, nearly all open timber trucks. Perhaps the worst feature of the operation of goods trains in Britain was the omission to provide them with continuous brakes. But either the private wagons would have to be equipped with these brakes — in some parts of the country, on two systems — or

the railway companies would have to buy them up and supply all wagons themselves. Sir John Aspinall of the Lancashire & Yorkshire once called private owners'
wagons "the bane of the English railways".

Although the British railways worked under conditions peculiar to themselves,
they learnt valuable lessons from abroad. G. J. Churchward, the very able Locomotive Engineer of the Great Western Company from 1902 to 1921, studied American practice closely, and imported three French compound engines to run side
by side with his own, which were simple. They did well; but the British conditions under which they worked – the very coal they burnt – were different from
the French, and Churchward decided in favour of the simple engine, cheaper to
construct and easier to drive. The imported engines offered no advantage from
compounding. They displayed a superiority in another respect, however: they
had four cylinders, each pair connected with a different pair of driving wheels,
and that distributed the blows of the pistons, to make these machines notably
steadier in running. So this divided drive, with four cylinders, became an essential
See Plate 23   element in Churchward's masterpiece for express work, the "Star" class, which
evolved in 1907–9. From America too he learnt valuable lessons, concerned with the
design of the front end of his locomotive. Presently he adopted and modified the
Schmidt superheater from Germany. All this experience went into the series of locomotives he produced at Swindon, standardised so that their boilers, wheels, etc.,
were built to a minimum number of sizes, and interchangeable. With his 4–6–0
express engines, his 2–6–0 for mixed traffic, and his 2–8–0 for heavy goods,
he set some of the highest standards of his time and helped to put the Great
Western back into the forefront, in speed and mechanical efficiency – a position it
had not occupied since the great days of Brunel and the young Daniel Gooch.

For all the unpopularity they had incurred, with politicians and commercial
men and labour, the railways had recovered something of the glamour, the
romance, they had inspired when they were new. Then they had entered as
exciting elements into the novels of Dickens and Surtees, into celebrated paintings
See Fig. 5   by Turner and Frith, into the unexcelled prints of Bourne. Now the sentiment
was of another kind; like that one might feel for an old friend, distinguished,
eccentric, and sometimes tiresome. Kipling expressed it beautifully in "The King"
in 1894:

> . . . "Romance!" the season-tickets mourn,
> "He never ran to catch His train,
> "But passed with coach and guard and horn –
> "And left the local – late again!
> "Confound Romance!" . . . and all unseen
> Romance brought up the nine-fifteen. . . .

There *was* now a romance about the railway. It emerged in the races to Scotland
in 1888 and 1895 – never intended as such, still less as devices for securing
publicity, though they became that. It found intelligent expression in Acworth's
Railways of England (1889), still the best general book ever written on the subject;

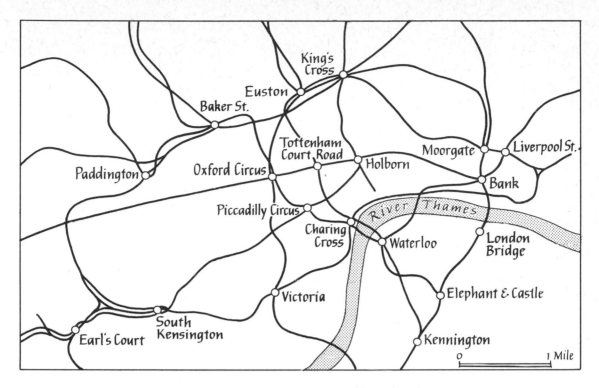

4   The Underground Railway system of Central London

and in the *Railway Magazine*, which began to appear in 1897 and has informed generations of readers ever since. In the new century the railways began to seek publicity, and to achieve it in useful forms. "The Cornish Riviera" – with all that idea came to mean for the economy of Cornwall – was a railway's phrase; at the bidding of the Great Northern Company an old salt appeared, capering on the sands of Skegness, and fixed that resort, hitherto not very prominent, firmly in people's minds. The railways assumed their place in the panoply of public cere- See Plate 22 monial: the royal trains conveying Queen Victoria and her son about the country; the funeral trains, richly caparisoned, that took them on their last journeys to Windsor. Foreigners coming to England – Americans arriving at Liverpool or Southampton and making for London, Europeans travelling up from Dover or Harwich – felt the impact of the railways immediately. They saw many things that were novel to them: the high platforms, the sparkling, bright-painted trains (what did a German think of a royal-blue locomotive, when he arrived at Liver- See Plate III pool Street?) – things no less odd than the double-deck motor-buses, the tubes, and the London police. The British railways had indeed a character that was their own, technical, economic, political, social. The British people had come to regard them much as they regarded the institutions of their country: without reverence, sometimes with exasperation, but affectionately and with pride.

The First World War

For the railways, as for Britain at large, an epoch ended with the outbreak of war in 1914. The task they faced in that war, and admirably performed, exhausted them, leaving them ill-equipped to meet profound changes that were already on the way before the war began.

They had little experience to build on – nothing like what the Germans had gained from their wars of 1864–70. The South African War in 1899–1902 had indeed required them to convey troops to and from the ports on a large scale. But that war had been fought in a remote country, and its direct impact upon the internal life of Britain had been small. An Engineer & Volunteer Staff Corps was in being, formed as far back as 1865. The army and the railways had flexed their muscles on a small scale in manoeuvres, notably those held throughout East Anglia in 1912. But now – all of a sudden, in August and September 1914 – an enemy established himself in the Low Countries, facing the Thames Estuary.

The mechanism had existed since 1871 to allow the Government to assume control of the railways when war broke out. Wisely, it left the business to railway-men, to a Railway Executive Committee consisting of the General Managers of the chief companies. The British Expeditionary Force was dispatched through Southampton: 69,000 men, 22,000 horses, 2,500 guns, with all their attendant baggage, in 334 trains, passed through in eight days of August. As many trains again followed during the rest of the month. Kitchener expressed his satisfaction generously: "The railway companies . . . have more than justified the complete confidence reposed in them by the War Office". The Commander-in-Chief acknowledged that every unit arrived in France "well within the scheduled time".

That was the first operation, and it became a continuous one throughout the five years that followed: to carry the troops overseas and bring them home. Soldiers made 9 million journeys through Folkestone in that time, 7 million through Southampton. The railways had also to provide for the conveyance of the wounded. When war broke out, plans had been drawn up for ambulance trains, converted from existing stock, but none had been built. Twelve were ready by the end of August 1914. First and last the British railways supplied 20 to run in Britain, together with 49 more for service overseas.

The hardest task did not fall wholly on the railways in the South. At the opposite end of the country the Highland Company had an equally difficult assignment, to maintain land communications with the two bases of the Grand Fleet in Cromarty Firth and Scapa Flow; difficult owing to the mountainous country through which its line passed, most of it single and all at the far end of a chain stretching from Perth 450 miles down to London. The work it performed lay out of the public eye; much of it indeed was top secret. The Northern Barrage minefield from Orkney to Norway was constructed largely from material landed by American ships at Kyle of Lochalsh on the west coast and transported thence by the steep and tortuous railway: 400 special trains were used in this work in six months of 1918.

The Highland Railway thus made a vital contribution, disproportionate to its size and strength, to the winning of the war at sea. But many other companies afforded assistance to the same end. The railways operated, taking them all together, a very large fleet of steamships. During the war the Government requisitioned 126 of them, 35 of which were lost, two-thirds off the coast of Britain, the rest between the Bay of Biscay and the White Sea.

Besides the conveyance of troops, the railways had another duty to perform, scarcely less important. This was to sustain the internal life of the country while the fighting raged abroad: to carry coal and food, to transport civilians on necessary (or even unnecessary) journeys. The Government did not take over the coal mines until 1916–17. When it did it appointed a railwayman to control them: Guy Calthrop, General Manager of the London & North Western Company. The facilities for civilian travel were curtailed but not cut off, except in those coastal districts to which access was limited. A few trifling branch lines were closed: on the South Eastern & Chatham the ten lines involved had an aggregate length of 24 miles. Though restaurant-car services were much reduced, they were never totally withdrawn: the Midland and the London & South Western Companies, for example, kept them going throughout the war. Though efforts were made to discourage travelling, they were not effective. Even the raising of fares by 50% at the beginning of 1917 and a drastic further reduction in service did not prove a deterrent.

The physical damage suffered by the railways from air raids was relatively slight. Two big London stations were hit: Liverpool Street (twice) and St Pancras. See Plate 33 There was little evidence of attack being directed against railway targets, except in a raid on Derby in 1916; and then the chief damage was repaired in two days.

Looking back, one may be inclined to think at first that this war made no very great impression on the railways. But that idea is wrong. Granted that the First World War was not as near to being "total" as the Second became, it taxed the railways' utmost resources, eating far into their reserves. And when it was over they were hit by two things at once: a stocktaking of the costs and a political inquest into their management.

During the war the Government guaranteed the railways the net receipts they had earned in 1913, to be divided among them in the proportions that had obtained in that year. But the war had produced a great inflation. Wages more than doubled, and so did the cost of many of the materials the railways used. Goods rates remained frozen at the level of 1913. The sole offset allowed during the war was the increase in passenger fares of 1917. When another railway strike occurred in 1919 it was settled through the intervention of the Government by a further increase in pay, which made the wages bill in 1920 three times what it had been before the war began. Goods rates were at length increased in the same year, and fares by another 25%. But those benefits turned out to be two-edged.

Though the Government made grants towards special maintenance costs arising from the war, all the railways were badly run down. The final compensation came through very slowly: £60 million, allotted between the companies.

Meanwhile, the railways were battling through a political storm. Some people had long urged that they should be purchased by the State. During the war the Government had imposed on the 130 companies it controlled many uniformities and a good deal of rationalisation. A pooling of most of the railway companies' wagons was accepted for example in 1917, and some progress was made towards bringing private owners' wagons into common use. When the Highland Company was short of locomotives, the Railway Executive Committee had been able to draft 20 to its aid from the other companies further south. Why should such valuable benefits cease with the war? Were not the railways one system, an instrument to serve the country's economy to the best advantage, in peacetime too?

Lloyd George's Coalition Government did not favour State control on any grounds of doctrine. But it was impressed by the benefits that seemed to have accrued from it during the war and wished to retain as many of them as possible. It sought a compromise between State ownership and private ownership on the old model; and the compromise it found in amalgamation, forcing the companies together into a small number of big units.

Lloyd George entrusted the work of realising the scheme to Sir Eric Geddes, who had been Deputy General Manager of the North Eastern Railway in 1914 and had shone in a number of administrative posts during the war. Geddes became the first Minister of Transport in 1919. He formulated his proposals without any consultation with the companies. So they were passed in an awkward way, with the least possible goodwill on both sides. Polite speeches had been made in 1918–19 about the railways' services during the war. As the Government's scheme was clamped down on the companies, those protestations looked extremely hollow.

The Railways Act that emerged in 1921 decreed the combination of 120 companies into four groups. The London underground railways were excluded from it altogether. One of the biggest of the old companies, the Great Western, remained little altered, though it absorbed the Cambrian and the railways in the valleys of South Wales. To the east of it the new Southern Railway combined the South Eastern & Chatham, the London Brighton & South Coast, and the London & South Western, to form a system based on London south of the Thames. The rest of England, and the whole of Scotland, was partitioned between two new companies: a London & North Eastern, reaching from the Thames to the Moray Firth; and, biggest of all, a London Midland & Scottish, which stretched out to Holyhead, Oban, and Wick.

Expressed in that summary form, the arrangements seem more rational than they were. The Government refused to dismember any of the existing companies, even if by some historical accident their lines strayed far into the territory of their neighbours. So in Wales the London Midland & Scottish was allowed to penetrate to Swansea, because the Midland and the North Western had done so; and the London & North Eastern was to be found, as successor to the Great Central, at Wrexham.

Those were anomalies, but, granted the principles on which the Act was drawn up, they could not have been avoided. The immediate anxiety of managements and shareholders was concentrated more on the financial terms of these mergers. What stock was to be received in the new companies, and at what price, in exchange for stock held in the old? Behind all these matters, however, lay something that was in the long run more important. Though the Government had decided against nationalisation, it had not abandoned all notions of State control. The Act strengthened its power to force the new companies to adopt plans of standardisation, co-operative working, and common user. And it set up a Railway Rates Tribunal with the object of controlling more closely than in the past, and on defined principles, the rates the companies charged. The declared objective was to enable them to earn a "standard revenue" based on that of 1913.

While all these plans were being debated, the Government kept the control of the railways it had assumed on the outbreak of war. It relinquished that control on the 15 August, the old companies then resumed their sway until the Railways Act went into force, from 1 January 1923.

Amalgamation

The new companies came into being at a difficult moment. It was fairly easy for the Great Western, which was not much altered by these arrangements; but in all the others there was, naturally, a struggle for power. The Southern came out of it well, for Sir Herbert Walker, who had been the General Manager of the London & South Western and was appointed to the same post with the new Company, was perhaps the outstanding railwayman of his time. He was soon able to devote himself to the electrification of suburban services, and here he could apply his own experience, gained through introducing them on the South
See Plate 44   Western. The work went ahead fast, and in 1925–6 a large programme was realised, taking electric traction out from London to Guildford, Sutton, Coulsdon, Orpington, and Dartford. The system adopted as standard was that of the South Western, using direct current from a third rail. The Brighton Company, however, had invested in an alternating-current overhead system. The Sutton and Coulsdon extensions followed that pattern, which allowed them to be completed quickly; but in 1928–9 the overhead system was superseded by the third rail, and the whole Southern installation became uniform.

This was the first stage in a much bigger task. With minor exceptions the suburban system was now all-electric. The second stage was announced in 1930: the electrification of the main line to Brighton and Worthing. It was completed in 1932. The process then went steadily further. By 1939 electric trains were running as far as Portsmouth, Hastings, Maidstone, and Gillingham.

Looking at the British railways in the final phase of private ownership, from 1923 to 1947, this electrification stands out clearly as their principal achievement. The London suburban railway system, the first in the world to grow densely, had then set hard in a mould. The Underground railways (electrified since 1905) were unexcelled. But many others were out of date, especially those of the South Eastern & Chatham. That Company had known what was needed. It secured powers to electrify in 1903 – and then left them unexercised. The amalgamation of 1923, and Walker's no-nonsense drive, enabled those plans to be realised swiftly. What resulted, taking the Southern lines and the Underground together, was an urban and suburban system no longer behind that of the rest of the world, but – given its intensity and peculiar problems – in many respects in front. The Southern's work may look easy to us now, the mere application of a formula. But it was much more than that. It called for high technical skill, constant ingenuity, and unswerving determination, and it was largely responsible for the increase of 25% in the railway's passenger traffic between 1923 and 1937.

Much of this traffic the railway created itself. When the Bexleyheath line was electrified, for example, it ran largely through open country. There is no open country at all on it now: it has helped to create a continuous suburb that stretches from London to Dartford. The creation may be good or bad – it is surely both; but whatever you think of it you must recognise that it is a social consequence first of the building and then of the electrification of the railway.

The two northern companies were bigger and more complex organisms than the Southern, and neither of them could have one objective, paramount over all others, like that programme of electrification. They had first to decide how to organise their work, stretched out over territories 600–700 miles long. They adopted different arrangements, which arose in part from their different histories.

The LNER based its organisation on accomplished facts. Shortly before the war the Great Central, Great Northern, and Great Eastern had tried to amalgamate, being prevented only by Parliament. They had much in common and could work in many respects easily as a sub-group. The North Eastern was already a monopoly, the only company in its large district (having absorbed the Hull & Barnsley in 1922); and the two Scottish companies, the North British and the Great North of Scotland, could form a natural partnership without friction. So the new Company determined to base its management on three areas, Southern, North Eastern, and Scottish, with a controlling high command in London. In practice this meant a considerable devolution of power.

The LMS decided on the opposite policy of concentration. There was much more rivalry and ill feeling among the companies that composed it: between the London & North Western and the Midland, between the Caledonian and the Glasgow & South Western. In all the companies created by the Act of 1921 there were intense personal jealousies, much jockeying for place; but these things were at their fiercest on the LMS. The new system was not only the biggest: it sprawled across Britain – reaching out an arm too into Ireland. Given these considerations, it became clear that the best hope of making the new company work would be through centralisation of control, under an autocracy, more or less benevolent. Having tried a looser, more liberal arrangement, the LMS searched for such an autocrat and found him in Josiah Stamp, who became President of the Executive (on the American model) in 1926 and remained in that post until he was killed in an air-raid 15 years later.

Of these two organisations the LNER settled into its task more smoothly, under an excellent Chief General Manager, Ralph Wedgwood. Financially, it was the weaker. The Great Central was in this respect a liability, the Great Eastern no strong asset – from the very nature of the country it served, rural East Anglia and the poorest part of London. When the slump came from 1929 onwards it hit north-eastern England with especial force, and the railways serving it fell on very hard times indeed. The LMS succeeded to more wealth: the London & North Western, the Midland, and the Lancashire & Yorkshire Companies had all been prosperous. It too was gravely damaged in the slump, notably on the Clyde and in Cumberland. But the structure it took over was stronger, and in this matter its task was less difficult.

What achievements stand out on the northern railways, to be placed beside that of the Southern? In electrification the LNER succeeded to a big plan for the North Eastern main line, which had got as far as an experimental stage; but that was dropped, and nothing of the sort appeared again until 1936. The LMS too inherited a scheme for electrification. When the Midland had taken over the London Tilbury & Southend Company in 1912 it had undertaken to electrify that system. It had failed to honour the promise, however, and its successor failed too. A little was done by the LMS in this way, in the Wirral and (jointly with the LNER) on the south side of Manchester; but there was no more. The Great Western (which had no problems of suburban traffic to solve, like those of the other three companies) confined itself to propounding a strangely-conceived plan for electrifying its main line from London to Penzance in 1938, abandoning it unregretted when the estimates of the cost came in.

One may feel impatient with the failure to seize this opportunity. But would large-scale electrification have been sensible then in Britain? She had no natural sources of hydro-electric power comparable with those of Alpine countries; and at the same time she was furnished with cheap and inexhaustible supplies of coal, including some of the best steam coal in the world. When that coal ceased to be cheap, a condition of British railway working that had been fundamental to it since 1825 disappeared, and it became necessary to look again at imported oil fuels and at electric power. The LMS began to develop the diesel shunting locomotive in 1934, and had rather more than 50 such machines in service at the time of nationalisation. The Great Western, which had used the steam railcar more than
See Plate 43 any other company, now took up the diesel railcar for passenger and parcels service and built 36 such units in 1934–42. Immediately after the war it turned to oil fuel for its steam locomotives, on an ambitious plan. This was favoured by the Government but then abandoned, not owing to technical failure but for lack of the foreign exchange needed to purchase the oil.

None of the companies could afford the capital cost of main-line electrification on a large scale. The Southern did it piecemeal, spreading the financial burden over 15 years, from 1924 to 1939. The LNER accepted the need to do the same with the lines out of Liverpool Street. Financially aided by the Government, and in collaboration with the Underground, it began the work in 1936. At the same time it also started the electrification of its lines from Manchester to Sheffield and Wath.

It would be untrue to say that no more could have been done in this direction. But for all the companies these were years of grave economic adversity. In 1923–6 they established themselves, caught up on the arrears they had suffered in the war, and began to improve their position. Then came the General Strike, which hit them hard. They started to recover from that and ran into the slump from 1929 onwards, and that hit them harder still. Again they struggled up out of deep depression, to be overshadowed by the threat of a second war, which came in 1939.

The causes of their financial difficulties were various, but one is outstanding: the growth of road competition. The petrol-driven vehicle had shown what it could do in 1914–18 – the services of the London "B" type bus on the Western Front were legendary. As soon as the war was over the buses came back to the roads and multiplied. Equally important, the goods lorry established itself, as it had hardly done before 1914: the number of them doubled in two years (1919–21) and doubled again in 1921–6. To some extent these buses and lorries were creating new traffic. What stood out, however, was that they were taking traffic off the railways.

The railways' response to this challenge was hesitant and slow. The Act of 1921 had been framed in part with a view to checking their monopoly. But that was a misconceived notion, hopelessly out of date: for they had a monopoly no longer. In comparison with their rivals, growing so fast, their services were dear (conspicuously dearer now, through the increase in fares and goods rates of 1917–20), and they were inflexible, from the nature of railways themselves as compared with roads.

Still, it remains true that the four railway companies failed, more completely than they need have done, to stand up to their new rivals. In country districts, for example, it was perfectly plain that the advantage lay with the bus. Until 1929 there were some legal obstacles to the railways going into the business of owning, or even investing in, bus undertakings; but they were not insuperable, and the big companies did little in this direction. Neither did they recognise their new situation squarely, and in the face of it withdraw. Only a minute frac-See Plate 47 tion of the railway system was abandoned – hardly more than 5% of that of the weakest of all these companies, the LNER. Here the railways might indeed have looked abroad and learnt a lesson: for this hard necessity was being faced in France. And even where it was accepted here, the French corollary of replacing the branch railway by a bus service connecting at the main-line station was not followed. In France some serious effort was made to retain an integrated transport system. Nothing of that kind appeared in Britain – except in one case; but that was notable indeed.

Almost all the tube railways of London, together with the District Company, had been brought together before the war into a single combine, which had also acquired the biggest of the bus companies, the General, in 1912. Only the Metropolitan Railway remained outside. In the years following the war bus competition in London, with the railways and with the General, became intense, increasing the already serious problem of traffic congestion. The London County Council, which was also in the transport business through its operation of a large tramway system, felt this competition too. By the mid-twenties proposals for planned co-ordination, or even a total merger, of the transport undertakings in London were being framed.

The upshot was the creation of the London Passenger Transport Board in 1933, a public corporation that owned all the Underground railways (including the Metropolitan), together with the tramways and bus services, whether they had been municipally or privately owned, within an area of nearly 2,000 square miles, from Hitchin to Crawley and from Slough to Gravesend. That did not quite create a monopoly, for the railways within this area that belonged to the four main-line companies remained in their hands. There was, however, to be a general pooling of receipts from the passenger traffic of them all.

The new Board represented an impressive endeavour: a long step towards establishing an integrated transport system for the largest city in the world. Aided by Government grants, the Board and two of the main-line companies pressed forward with important joint schemes for extending the Underground system. None of them was quite complete before the war started; but in 1939–41 tube trains began to run out to Stanmore, Barnet, and Mill Hill. Two other schemes, under way at the same time, were temporarily abandoned in 1940. They were realised soon after the war was over.

Besides their railways, the Underground and the Board have left behind them two notable memorials: in the long series of their posters, which raised the standard of publicity to a level hardly attained by any other transport under- taking anywhere, before or since; and in the stations designed for them by Charles Holden, or under his influence, especially those on the Piccadilly line See Plate 46 extensions of 1932–3, like Arnos Grove. Here the British railways offered out- standing examples of the twentieth-century railway station, impressive at once functionally and in design. But none of the main-line companies paid attention to what the London railways had done. The Great Western and the Southern rebuilt a number of their stations – Leamington and Cardiff, for instance, Exeter (Queen Street) and Surbiton. In each case this produced a great improvement in convenience but an architecture that, at the kindest, can only be called undistin- guished. At one point, and at one only, something remarkable emerged: in the Midland Hotel at Morecambe, which the LMS Company commissioned from Oliver Hill and built in 1932–3. This was no reconstruction, but an entirely new building in the most forward-looking manner of the time: a thing hardly to be matched then, on this scale, anywhere else in Great Britain.

Here were some signs that the railways were anxious not only to improve their services but to draw attention to them. There were others, and of them the most spectacular were the high-speed trains of the 1930s. The LNER did most in See Plate 48 this business, with its "Silver Jubilee" of 1935, running from London to New- castle in four hours, followed by similar trains to Edinburgh and to the West Riding of Yorkshire in 1937. Its rival the LMS Company put on a corresponding service in the same year from Euston to Glasgow in 6½ hours – where the previous time had been 7½. Special locomotives and rolling-stock were used for all these trains, streamlined throughout. They made a powerful impression. These four trains were a sign that Britain intended to keep the lead she had so long enjoyed among European countries in the provision of express service. And as long as trains continued to be hauled by the power of steam, she did.

The Pacific (4–6–2) locomotives used on these super-expresses were, on both railways, a development from types that had been evolving for some time past. On the LNER Nigel Gresley had been steadily improving his first Pacific of 1922. He had made important changes in it, in the setting of the cylinder valves and in the boiler pressure, as a result of competitive trials of his machines held against "Castle" class engines of the Great Western in 1925. In its ultimate streamlined form, one of his Pacifics, *Mallard*, captured the world's speed record for a steam locomotive, of 126 m.p.h., in 1938. The posthumous influence of Churchward thus percolated far from his works at Swindon.

It extended also to the LMS, for William Stanier, who became the Company's Chief Mechanical Engineer in 1932, was a Swindon man by training; and the Pacific locomotives he designed for his new company reflected that earlier experience, especially in their boilers. The influence is to be noted; but one must not exaggerate its importance. Gresley and Stanier were notable engineers in their own right. The locomotives they designed, and then patiently improved, were, like all such machines, the fruit of experience observed – everywhere, on their own railways, on the Great Western, in America – shaped by their individual qualities and talents. It must be added that Stanier faced a formidable task when he went to the LMS, for he took over an enormous fleet of widely-assorted loco-motives, most of them old-fashioned, under-powered, and expensive in service. The standard types he evolved proved highly successful, and it was largely on them that British Railways based the design of their engines after nationalisa-tion.

These were difficult years indeed for the railways, years of disappointment, frustration, and missed opportunity. In that their history reflects the history of Britain. Not all their opportunities were missed, however; and to judge them fairly one must remember that their work was cut short, leaving much promise unfulfilled, by the outbreak of war in 1939.

The Second War and its Aftermath

The Second World War, unlike the First, did not hit Britain suddenly. With every year that had passed since 1933 the chances of war had obviously in-creased; the crisis of 1938 had shown that it could hardly be avoided. The immediate danger of heavy attack from the air was now much greater, and in September 1939 one of the railways' first tasks was to convey children and their mothers away from the big towns. During that month they moved 1,300,000, half of them from London and the South-East, in nearly 4,000 special trains.

See Plate 49

This was the biggest single operation of the kind, but it was only one among several during the next five years. It was repeated for example in 1940, and in 1944 under the attack from flying bombs.

The railways did much for the civilian population in another way too. Some Underground stations had been used as deep-level shelters during the first war. In the second they became an essential part of the defence of London. Seventy-nine stations were, eventually, fitted up with bunks and other necessary facilities, which could between them accommodate up to 75,000 people – in grave emergency, even more – every night. In the whole course of the war the tubes took in 63 million shelterers.

See Plate 50

The first bomb fell on a railway on 19 June 1940; the last on 27 March 1945. In the course of that time 900 people were killed by enemy action on the railways, 4,000 carriages and wagons destroyed – but no more than eight locomotives. About 9,000 "incidents" occurred altogether, 250 of which were so serious as to interrupt traffic for more than a week. The destruction was far graver than in the first war. Yet it was much less than the corresponding destruction in Germany, or in France and the Low Countries in 1944–5; less too than the Germans themselves intended and hoped.

That is partly to be explained by pure chance. What else was it when, on 16 October 1939, a raiding aircraft secured a hit on a cruiser lying close to the Forth Bridge but missed the bridge itself? It was also due in large measure to the devoted tenacity of the railwaymen, which often rose to heroism and sometimes even above that: in the handling of wagons loaded with ammunition, for example at Breck Road, Liverpool, in May 1941, and at Soham (saving a large part of that little town from destruction) on 2 June 1944. Or think of the calm of the signalmen at London Bridge and Charing Cross, with land-mines hitched to their signal-boxes, refusing to leave because their duty had still to be done. Three George Crosses and twenty-nine George Medals were won on the railways during the war.

The military traffic carried in the second war differed in some ways from that of 1914–18. The first Expeditionary Force, to France in 1939, was conveyed much as its predecessor had been 25 years before – a third as many men again, but this time without horses. The second, to Norway in April 1940, required 200 special trains running to Leith and Glasgow. They were put on at very short notice. There was no notice at all of the next great demand on the railways: to bring back the troops evacuated from Dunkirk. A total of 620 journeys were made for this purpose, conveying 319,000 men. It was an outstanding achievement in improvisation. The cool official history remarks: "for this masterly handling of train movements the railways fully deserved the credit they received".

No suddenly improvised operation of that kind had to be mounted again. The dispatch of troops to North Africa in 1942 went to a predetermined schedule. So did the re-entry into Europe, with the Normandy landings in 1944. This was by far the biggest undertaking of the sort that the British railways had ever handled. For one purpose or another, the railways ran 524,000 trains on the

Government's account between September 1939 and June 1945. More than half of those travelled in the final 18 months.

In this second war, as in the first, the railways' manufacturing plant was used extensively for the making of munitions. The LMS turned out 642 tanks from Horwich and Crewe; Derby repaired Hampden and Lancaster bombers. Necessarily, such tasks as these were performed at the expense of the works' proper business. It became very hard to keep an adequate number of locomotives, carriages, and wagons in repair, and the difficulty was increased by Government demands of every kind. In September 1941, for example, the railways were told they must give up 151 of their best freight engines, to be sent to Persia. Next year the supply of locomotives became critically insufficient: on one day nearly 30% of the heavy goods engines of the LNER were found to be out of service. But the crisis was surmounted in 1943. A number of the "Austerity" 2–8–0 locomotives produced by the Government for military use were lent to the railways, together with 400 similar machines from the United States. Nevertheless, labour in the shops and running sheds remained very scarce, and the difficulties of maintenance were unending.

The Government's control of the railways in the second war was exercised in much the same way as before. It promised, when it took them over, to pay them the revenues they had earned, on average, in the three years 1935–7. This time, however, a margin was allowed, within which the railways might retain any further profits they made; beyond that margin, the Government was to take everything. These arrangements were subsequently revised in favour of a fixed payment. The Railway Executive Committee reappeared. From 1941 it was under the chairmanship not of a railwayman but of a "Controller of Railways", Sir Alan Anderson, a businessman who had formerly been a railway director. The Government assumed a closer control of the railways than in the first war; and necessarily, because the second war affected the nation's life much more directly and completely. Its part was confined to policy, however: the execution of the policy was left to the railways themselves.

Besides meeting military demands, the railways had to keep the ordinary traffic of the country going. Many efforts were made to reduce civilian travel. Two increases of fares were imposed in 1940; but there were no more. Long-distance passenger journeys multiplied notably. Railway travel was permitted even to race-meetings, at Ascot and Newmarket for example in 1944, provoking strong public criticism. Various plans were considered for rationing railway travel, and rejected either as impracticable or as imposing unnecessary hardship. The Government had a delicate balance to hold. It remained the strong and sole arbitrator.

The burden of the war was not distributed in the same way, between the railway systems, as in 1914–18. From air-raids, the Southern Railway and London Transport suffered most. In terms of operation, the worst difficulties arose perhaps on the Great Western, to whose area so much of the business of the country had shifted as a result of the air attacks on the South-East. The Severn Tunnel was a

III   2–4–0 mixed traffic locomotive, class T26, designed by James Holden for the Great Eastern Railway. A hundred of the type were built between 1891 and 1902. This one is in the National Railway Museum at York.

IV   The ultimate evolution of the standard British 4–4–0 express engine (see p. 81): the "Director" class, designed by J. G. Robinson for the Great Central Railway. Twenty-one were built from 1913 onwards to work the express trains between Marylebone, Sheffield, and Manchester. The LNER built a further 24 for service in Scotland. This machine has also been preserved.

narrow bottleneck, quite irremoveable. Every coal train worked through it, plunging (loose-coupled) down the gradient at one end and then toiling steeply up the other, displaced three faster-moving passenger trains. About £6½ million pounds were spent on improvements to the railway system during the war — mainly on the provision of additional tracks and sidings. Nearly half that sum went on the Great Western: on a marshalling yard at Oxford, for instance, on quadrupling the line between Gloucester and Cheltenham (jointly owned with the LMS), on doubling the single line between Didcot and Newbury, on improving the engine sheds and on a housing scheme at Severn Tunnel Junction.

When it was all over, a Labour Government was returned to power, committed to extensive nationalisation, with the railways in the front of the programme. This great change was brought about more rapidly than the corresponding and smaller one of 1921. Again it was imposed on the railways, without consulting their chairmen or managers: with better reason this time, for the policy was evidently unacceptable to them, and it was certain to be realised because the Government enjoyed a large and secure majority in Parliament. The Transport Act of 1947 laid down that the railways were to be purchased by the State. It applied not to the main-line companies alone but also to the London Passenger Transport Board and to a few surviving "independents". It was designed to establish an integrated system for the whole country, extending to road and water transport as well as to railways, under public ownership. The success and failure of this endeavour are a theme of the next chapter.

11   The broad gauge on the Great Western Railway. *Lightning*, one of the first series of Daniel Gooch's 4–2–2 express engines, built in 1847. The hooded iron seat at the back of the tender was for a porter, whose duty it was to keep the train under observation.

12   Sydney Gardens, Bath. The elegant design of the masonry matched its surroundings. An express is entering from the east. Note the "mixed-gauge" track.

13 Broad-gauge locomotives waiting to be scrapped at Swindon after the final conversion in 1892. In front is a row of the express engines.

14 Building the Metropolitan Railway along Praed Street, with the Great Western Hotel at Paddington prominent in the background.

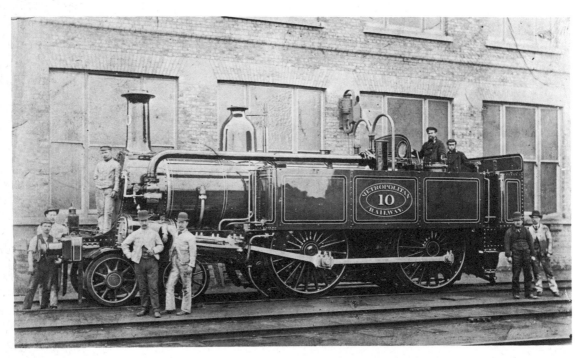

15 Steam locomotive of the Metropolitan Railway. This was the only type used on the Inner Circle until 1905, when it was converted to electric traction.

16 Huddersfield station (architect, J. P. Pritchett), completed in 1849. A very rare example in Britain of a station treated as a civic building. The great length of the front is not merely ostentatious. The station was "single-sided", the whole of the passenger traffic being accommodated at one platform 700 ft. long, into which trains ran from both directions. The building and the square in front were excellently refurbished in the early 1970s.

17 Mid-Victorian Gothic: Great Malvern station (architect, E. W. Elmslie), 1861.

18   Paisley (Gilmour Street) station. The building on the left, projecting from it at a right angle, is the Post Office – indicating the close collaboration between the railways and the postal service.

19   Shipping locomotives at Birkenhead for export, *c.* 1875.

20　A late and successful example of the express locomotive with single driving wheels: one of a type of which 95 were built for the Midland Railway in 1887–1900. These machines remained in service long after almost all others of their kind had gone. The last was withdrawn in 1928 and has been preserved. In their crimson-lake livery they were surely among the most elegant locomotives ever built.

21　*Dunalastair*, J. G. McIntosh's 4–4–0 for the Caledonian Railway (1896), the first British express engine to be fitted with a really large boiler.

22 Royal train near Ballater, Great North of Scotland Railway, 1910.

23 Great Western locomotive 4005 *Polar Star* at Euston, on trial on the London & North Western Railway, 1910. *Worcestershire*, an "Experiment" locomotive of the LNWR, worked at the same time on the GWR.

24 The first motor-buses operated by a main-line railway in Britain ran in Cornwall. They were the Great, Western's, from the station at Helston to the Lizard; the service started in Aug. 1903.

25 The North Eastern and the Lancashire & Yorkshire Railways handled goods traffic by road motor vehicles on a considerable scale. Here is one of the North Eastern's lorries.

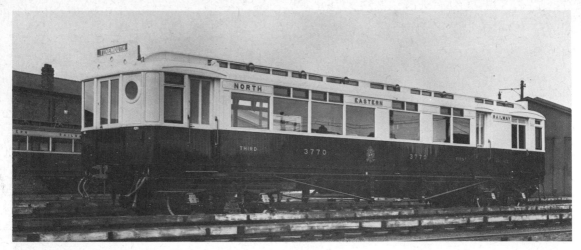

26 Composite motor-car for the Tyneside electric service of the North Eastern Railway, inaugurated in 1904.

27 London & North Western steam rail-motor (cf. p. 69). The locomotive is enclosed in the body of the vehicle at the far end. Steps are provided for use at halts with low platforms.

28 Tube train at Hampstead, 1910.

29 Great Yarmouth: the Hall Quay, *c.* 1900. The locomotive is one of the Great Eastern Railway "tram engines" fitted with a cowcatcher and with its motion enclosed to allow it to work on public roads.

30 The paddle steamer *Glen Sannox*, built for the Glasgow & South Western Railway in 1892, approaching Brodick Pier, Arran, in LMS days. When the ship was new she took part in operating a service, against the competition of the Caledonian, that brought the time from Glasgow to Brodick down to 80 minutes. (The journey today, at its quickest, takes about half as long again.) It was a costly, insensate rivalry for what was always a quite small traffic.

31 The traditional type of British goods wagons: timber-built, open, with hand brakes. These belonged to the Swansea Harbour Trust. Photograph taken in 1925.

32 Coal waiting for shipment: Swansea Docks, 1906. Private owners' wagons alone are to be seen in the picture (cf. p. 83).

33 Signal-box at Streatham Common, London Brighton & South Coast Railway, destroyed in an air raid, 1916.

34 Women were employed extensively by railways in the First World War. Here are two ticket collectors on the London & South Western at Waterloo.

35, 36 Saloon carriage taken over by the Great Western from the Brecon & Merthyr Company, photographed in 1924 after it had been taken out of service.

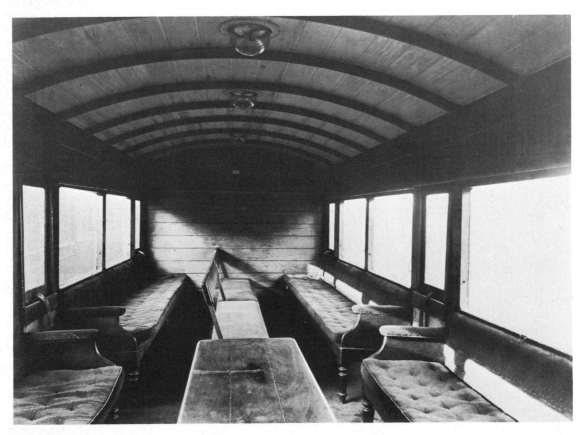

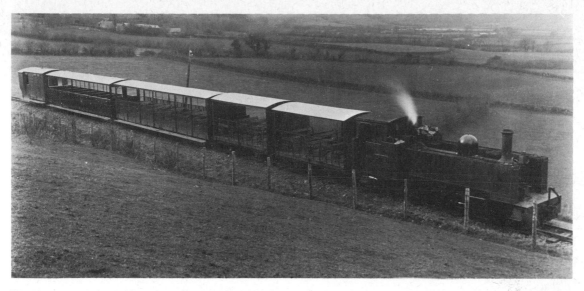

37 Narrow gauge in Wales: the Vale of Rheidol line from Aberystwyth to the Devil's Bridge. Open-sided carriages, for scenic observation. 2–6–2 tank locomotive, built by Davies & Metcalfe of Romiley, Cheshire, 1902. The picture dates from 1923, and the engine bears its Great Western number, 1213.

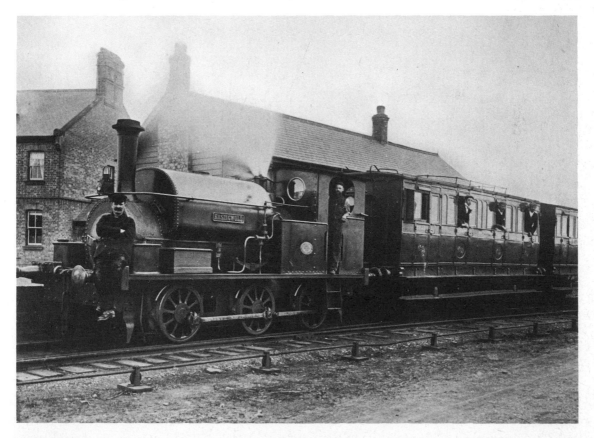

38 The Easingwold was one of the smallest railway companies in Britain: the entire system comprised the $2\frac{1}{2}$ m. line from Easingwold down to the York–Newcastle line at Alne. It was open in 1891 and had a surprisingly prosperous existence for a long time. It was closed in 1957. This locomotive worked on the line from 1891 to 1903.

39 The signal gantry east of Newcastle Central station in early LNER days, c. 1925.

40 The 100th anniversary of the Stockton & Darlington Railway was celebrated by the LNER on 27 Sept. 1925. A long series of locomotives and trains passed before the spectators at Darlington. Here is a train of the Great North of Scotland Company, headed by a "K" class locomotive built in 1866.

41   Removal of the complete stock and equipment of a farm in Scotland, *c.* 1925.

42   Loch Awe: Ford Pier, with LMS bus connecting with the small steamer.

43 Great Western Railway diesel railcar No. 2. This was one of three built in 1934 with small buffets to work an express service between Birmingham and South Wales. The Company built 38 diesel railcars, for different types of service, in 1934–42.

44 Southern Electric. The front three-coach set is made up of converted South Eastern & Chatham Railway steam stock; the next two coaches come from the London Brighton & South Coast.

45 A new ancillary undertaking developed by the railways was Railway Air Services, notable as a partnership between all four main-line companies. Its most successful service was between Bristol and Cardiff.

46 Arnos Grove, one of the distinguished series of stations designed for the London Underground and built in 1932–3.

116

47   The nineteenth century projecting itself far into the twentieth. Here is a "push-and-pull" train operating on the Palace Gates branch of the LNER as it had done in the Victorian age, though with superior rolling-stock. Note the provision of three classes of accommodation.

48   The streamlined "Silver Jubilee" express of the LNER (cf. p. 94), introduced in 1935.

49   Evacuation, 1940: a scene on the LNER.

50   The wreckage at York after the air-raid of 29 Apr. 1942. Gresley Pacific locomotive *Sir Ralph Wedgwood* lying destroyed in the foreground.

3. The Nationalised Railways 1948-75

In the 27 years since nationalisation, the railways of Great Britain have experienced more radical changes than in any equivalent period of their history, save perhaps the great era of expansion between 1840 and 1870. The system has shrunk from 20,000 route-miles to 11,500. The staff has been reduced from over 640,000 to about a third of that figure. Steam traction has disappeared and been replaced by electric and diesel haulage. Changes in organisation, and also relationships with other forms of transport, both publicly-owned and privately-owned, have been almost incessant throughout the whole period. Both as seen by the Government and the general public, the role of the railways has fundamentally altered.

Four different periods in the quarter-century since nationalisation can be identified, each characterised by an emphasis on some particular ingredient of change. To a large extent these periods were marked by the passage of Acts of Parliament, each of which gave expression to new Government thinking about how railways should be organised, and their role in a modern economy.

Railway Unification and "Integrated" Transport

The first period started at midnight on 31 December 1947, when engine whistles were sounded by the drivers of the night trains to celebrate the beginning of national ownership. For a considerable time, however, the public did not detect much change, apart from the appearance of the legend "British Railways" on the tenders of locomotives and on public notices. But Dr Hugh Dalton, the then Chancellor of the Exchequer, in an unguarded moment said publicly that by taking over the railways the State had acquired "a poor bag of assets". This statement was widely resented in the industry, where it was pointed out that the condition of the railways was mainly due to the continuance of Government controls over charging long after they had ceased to be applicable with the growth of mechanical road transport. This had produced inability to earn profits or to attract new capital for modernisation. There had also been Government decisions that the railways must carry the brunt of the wartime traffics without being permitted adequate replacement of track, locomotives, and rolling-stock, and that the profits which would normally have been earned from the enormous wartime traffics were not to be retained by the railways.

It is worth examining, after a quarter of a century, the validity of Dr Dalton's criticism. The railways were certainly something of an exhausted giant in 1948. Staff morale was not good, except for a proportion of the older railwaymen who had carried on the best traditions of the industry during and after the war. Track was in no state for the resumption of the high-speed trains of the pre-war era; and, whilst the wagon fleet had received fairly substantial additions during the war, mainly of mineral wagons, the passenger rolling-stock and the locomotives were urgently in need of replacements. Stations were shabby and many had been damaged by enemy action. Signalling and telecommunications urgently needed major modernisation and renewals. Even so, the assets in the "poor bag" included some £178 million of marketable securities, mostly representing arrears of maintenance provisions, and £24 million in war damage claims.

The Companies even before the end of the war had begun to prepare their own plans for overtaking the arrears of maintenance. The Labour Government was not, however, much interested in any proposals from the Companies pending the passing of the Transport Act, 1947, which nationalised not merely the railways but also London Transport, the canals, and the railway-owned docks; and which placed these under a British Transport Commission given extensive powers to prepare schemes for acquiring all other forms of public inland transport, including road passenger and road freight undertakings, and other ports and harbours. From the start, the fact that the railways became merely one of several Executives of the British Transport Commission created problems both of organisation and personal relationships which were not solved for a considerable time.

The most immediate result of the Act was that the four main-line railway Companies, as well as nearly all the minor railways, ceased to exist and were placed under the Railway Executive, which described its undertaking as "British Railways" for commercial and publicity purposes. The Railway Executive created six "Regions", largely but not entirely based on the systems of the former Companies, namely the Eastern, London Midland, North Eastern, Scottish, Southern and Western Regions. The major difference between the former Company boundaries and the Regional boundaries was that Scotland was cut off from the former LMS and LNER systems and formed into an independent unit; and the LNER was broken into two components, roughly corresponding to the North Eastern and Southern Areas of the former LNER. Various adjustments were, however, made to reduce the extent of inter-Regional penetration and establish more compact territories; for example, the former London Tilbury & Southend line of the LMS Railway was transferred to the Eastern Region of British Railways.

The Railway Executive, which became the central management for British Railways, was in many ways a peculiar body. Although its Members were appointed by the Minister and it was treated as the employer of the staff and had the power to enter into contracts, technically it was merely an agent of the British Transport Commission, which was the owner of the whole business. The Executive in fact could only function under a Scheme of Delegation by which the Commission passed certain powers to it.

The first Chairman of the Commission was Sir Cyril (later Lord) Hurcomb, whilst the Executive was at the outset placed under the Chairmanship of the former General Manager of the Southern Railway, Sir Eustace Missenden. Most of its Members, each of whom had charge of a group of departments, were former Company Chief Officers.

The first task of the Executive was to transform the Company organisations into Regional offices. Old loyalties were still strong and the Executive did not always find it easy to override these. The Regions were not allowed to have General Managers of their own; the departmental officers in the Regions reported direct to the appropriate departmental Member of the Railway Executive, and the only representative of general management in the Regions was a Chief Regional Officer whose powers were rather to co-ordinate than to control.

The Railway Executive saw its first task as being to review the physical state of the business. In the first Annual Report of the British Transport Commission the Executive claimed that, despite the fact that there were heavy arrears of maintenance and normal wear and tear as well as war damage to deal with, it was not making the mistake of assuming that one must simply replace what had existed before. Its approach was, in its own words, "to measure the existing assets against the requirements of 1948 and later years, under conditions of transport unification".

Many wartime controls still existed in 1948; for instance, a form of rationing was in force for key materials and certain types of labour. The Executive, however, considered that a unified system, as compared with four companies employing different standards and practices, ought to produce substantial savings and (in the long term) improved efficiency. It made a study of what it termed the "ideal" stocks of locomotives and wagons, based on this concept of rationalising requirements. As a first instalment, it proposed to get rid of some 85,000 elderly mineral wagons lubricated with grease instead of with oil axle-boxes. Modernisation of the collection and delivery services was also needed – in 1948 British Railways still had 7,000 horses engaged in this work and mechanisation was far from complete.

Meanwhile, the post-war traffic pressure on the railways continued. Road transport was far from recovering anything like its pre-war position. The Armed Forces continued to travel in very large numbers. The main concern of the Executive was with freight traffic, particularly the movement of coal to power stations; improvement of passenger services had necessarily to take a lower priority. Locomotives were still in poor condition, often leaking steam at every gland; and the absence of coal of pre-war quality meant that they steamed poorly and lost time even on the slower schedules still in force.

From 1948 onwards the railways continually urged on the Government, through the British Transport Commission, the need for adequate investment to bring their system into a state of physical efficiency. The controls on investment at that date were not financial but (continuing a war-time practice) were expressed in terms of the key factors in short supply. For some years the Investment Programmes Committee, then the Government's co-ordinating authority, consistently gave higher priority to the fuel and power industries, particularly coal and electricity, with steel following closely behind. The railways were in effect told that they would have to "live off their fat" for a few more years. The Government was unwilling to recognise that the "fat" had practically all disappeared.

Writing after his retirement from the position of Chairman and General Manager of the Eastern Region, D. S. M. Barrie remarked of this period that

it took many railroad men, including some of the most senior, some time to realise that the political act of nationalisation implied almost a new dimension in the industry's relations with the public. Services were late to recover in speed and reliability towards the splendid pre-war standards; there were many more complaints, and now there were statutory bodies to whom they could be made. Members of the party not in power, newspaper writers and many members of the public, attributed shortcomings solely to nationalisation. Resentment and some cynicism grew amongst the staff.

Even so, despite physical shortages and some discontent, progress continued with technical standardisation in practically all the departmental functions. Committees were set up at Railway Executive headquarters, composed of officers of the former Companies and now of the Regions, to examine the differences in practice, to compare their advantages and disadvantages, and make recommendations for single future standards for British Railways as a whole. The Railway Executive also introduced a standard pattern of organisation in the Regions, sweeping away individual Company practices.

There were two new factors to which railway managers had to adapt themselves after nationalisation. One was the consultative procedure, under which their actions had to be justified to bodies allegedly representing the public but bearing no financial or commercial responsibilities, in the form of Transport Users' Consultative Committees. The other was the disillusionment experienced by organised railway labour after nationalisation. The staff found that the efforts of the Railway Executive to introduce standardised forms and procedures meant a flood of new instructions, some of which were either unintelligible or objectionable to both staff and managers, who implemented them with little enthusiasm.

Staff relations were, however, improved by the establishment in 1949 of a Joint Consultation procedure by agreement with the Unions, which was supplementary to and quite apart from the machinery for negotiation of railway wages and conditions. And, despite its difficulties, the Executive did manage to effect a gradual improvement in the quality of railway services. Trains were speeded up, as and when the tracks were restored to something approaching pre-war standards; named trains were re-introduced and restaurant- and buffet-car services were increased. The repainting and repair and reconstruction of passenger stations for a time lagged behind.

There had been two main reasons, apart from pure political theory, for nationalising the greater part of all public inland transport in 1948. The first was to improve efficiency and economy by unifying the four main-line railways and introducing standard practices, eliminating overlapping and waste. This was achieved with some measure of success by the Railway Executive. The second objective, the responsibility of the Transport Commission, was "integration" of public inland transport. Here the aim was to reduce overall costs by eliminating the competition between road and rail which, particularly in the freight field, was claimed to be both wasteful and unfair — wasteful, because the erosion of railway traffic by road transport had meant that effective railway capacity was not being fully utilised, whilst heavy new investment was flowing into building new highways and new road vehicles; unfair, because the diversion of traffic from rail to road was assisted by the outmoded and rigid charging system, with publication of rates, imposed on the railways by Parliament. Road transport was entirely free in its charging methods; this enabled it to abstract traffic by the simple process of ascertaining the published railway rate for any particular traffic, and then undercutting that rate by what was necessary to secure the business. To remedy this the Labour Government pinned its faith on integration, to be achieved by bringing the railways and road transport into public ownership with unified control at the top level.

The railway Unions saw integration as making sense only if it achieved protection of rail traffic from road competition. But the Government and the British Transport Commission saw clearly that compulsion, involving the direction of traffic, would be intensely unpopular with the public and with industry. Integration was therefore intended to be approached through the manipulation of charges rather than by direct restriction. Under the 1947 Act it became the Commission's responsibility to prepare Charges Schemes; and within a few weeks of nationalisation the Commission set out to implement this task.

The Railway Executive, however, was meanwhile devoting relatively little attention to integration; much more to internal reforms. The Executive was composed of Members who, although having collective responsibility for decisions of the Executive as a whole, regarded their main tasks as being those of departmental chiefs, with teams of officers working beneath them. Members of the Executive also tended, naturally enough, to select their Headquarters Chief Officers from their own former Companies. Thus the design standards and thinking of the Executive in the different functions tended initially to be influenced by the practices of one former Company, according to the origins of the Member concerned.

Nevertheless, various fact-finding bodies were set up to consider the existing practices on the Regions, inherited from the Companies, and to compare the advantages and disadvantages of each with a view to evolving the best future standard. This policy produced the steam locomotive interchange trials of 1948, in which former Company designs of locomotives were tested against each other on unfamiliar routes and their performance and coal consumption carefully studied. The trials aroused enormous interest. In some ways they were probably one of the best advertisements for nationalisation, since they showed the possibility of taking an entirely new look at, for example, the steam locomotive in unfamiliar surroundings. There was not of course quite the same competitive atmosphere as in earlier exchange trials, such as those in 1925 between the former GWR and the LNER, which had amounted almost to a national sporting event.

Following the 1948 interchange trials, the Railway Executive developed new standard designs of steam locomotive, ten in all being planned. The object was to reduce the number of types, reduce the stock of spares and simplify maintenance procedures. Having regard to the fact that the Executive had inherited some 20,000 locomotives, of 448 different types, with an average life of perhaps 35 years, and with the lessons already learnt in the United States and on the Continent about diesel and electric traction, this policy now seems with hindsight to have been over-conservative. The new designs, with a flavour of LMS practice, began to appear progressively, from the emergence of the 4–6–2 "Britannia" express passenger type in 1951 to the last steam locomotive built for BR, the 2–10–0 freight locomotive *Evening Star*, in 1960.

The same policy of standardisation was followed in respect of carriages and wagons. By 1950 designs had been completed for 12 types of standard all-steel gangway passenger coaches; and an experimental double-decker train for suburban traffic on the Southern Region was put into service in 1949. New third-class sleeping cars with only two berths in a compartment and full bedding accommodation and washing facilities were introduced in 1952. The Executive also set up a committee to make a comprehensive review of the design and capacity of types of wagons, covering the complete elimination of the grease-lubricated wagons taken over from the private owners; the pros and cons of fitting automatic brakes to all freight wagons; the comparative merits of vacuum and air brakes for freight stock; and the type of coupling to be adopted. Acquisition of the former privately-owned freight wagons was also completed. Some 544,000 wagons were bought up, at a total cost in excess of £42m. But by 1953 development of a 24½-ton mineral wagon on two axles was in hand, the largest wagon that can be built without changing to a bogie design.

Two electrification schemes that had been suspended during the war were restarted, one from Liverpool Street to Shenfield, completed in September 1949, the other from Manchester to Sheffield and Wath, completed by 1954. In the first nine months after the opening of the Liverpool Street–Shenfield electrification, passenger journeys were up by 49·5% compared with the corresponding period of the previous year. This encouraged the Eastern Region to embark on preliminary planning for extensions of suburban electrification covering the remaining lines radiating from Liverpool Street and also the London Tilbury & Southend line from Fenchurch Street. Electrification of the heavily-used Enfield and Chingford lines was something that had been considered by the former Great Eastern Railway 30 years before and therefore naturally appeared as a long overdue instalment of modernisation. But the decision to execute these schemes had to wait until more substantial funds could be released to the railways for modernisation.

Progress towards the full adoption of diesel and electric traction was slow. Here the unfortunate consequences of dividing responsibility between the British Transport Commission and the Railway Executive were apparent. In April 1948 the Chairman of the BTC wrote to the Railway Executive asking that a Committee on motive power should be set up, to study not the technical features of steam, diesel and electric traction, but the economics of these forms in relation to future traction demands on the railways; and to lay down a policy. The Railway Executive eventually set up a Committee at the end of 1948 which did not report until October 1951. The Committee proposed only one pilot main-line electrification scheme and a test of diesel traction for main-line duties, expanding the small-scale experiment that had been taking place over the past three years with a handful of diesel locomotives and two unsuccessful gas-turbine locomotives. But the Committee had no hesitation in recommending an extension of the policy already in force on several Regions of using diesel locomotives for shunting, for which purpose they had proved reliable and economical. The Committee also proposed that a scheme for introducing modern diesel railcars on a large scale should be studied. The Railway Executive adopted only a minor part of these recommendations; main-line diesel traction and main-line electrification schemes still had to wait.

See Plate 52

Mention should be made here of the position of the London Underground railways which, though belonging to the London Transport Executive and not British Railways, can claim some ancestral links with the Stockton & Darlington Railway. Before the war, co-operation between the four main-line Companies and the London Passenger Transport Board had been close. A major result of this co-operation had been the promotion of the New Works Programme, 1935–40, by the LPTB and the main-line railway Companies, which was financed by Government guarantees on stock issued at a very low rate of interest in order to relieve unemployment.

There was an extensive programme of Underground railway developments, involving co-operation between LNER, GWR, and the LPTB, to promote extensions of the Tube network over inner suburban routes of the main line railways. In the early part of the war substantial parts of this programme were brought into use, affecting the Metropolitan line to Stanmore and the former LNER lines to High Barnet and Mill Hill East; the remainder was deferred. When it was resumed, the London Transport Central Line services were projected eastwards in 1947–48 as far as Woodford, Loughton, and Hainault, and in the west to West Ruislip over the Western Region. The project was completed by electrification of the Eastern Region tracks between Loughton and Epping in 1949, and from Epping to Ongar in 1957.

One section of the projected Tube services, that from Finsbury Park, Crouch End and Highgate to Alexandra Palace, was considered to be no longer economically justified in the light of post-war changes in the traffic pattern, so the electrification of this branch of the former LNER was abandoned.

Quite separately from the 1935–40 New Works Programme, there had been set up in 1944, following the County of London Plan 1943 (the Forshaw/Abercrombie Report), a Government-sponsored Railway (London Plan) Committee which was required to make proposals for transport development in London under peacetime conditions. This Committee proposed a network of new cross-London underground railways, some constructed to the smaller "Tube" loading gauge and some constructed to the main-line loading gauge. The total expenditure involved in these grandiose schemes can be fairly described as astronomical; and the physical resources required to carry out the works would almost certainly have overstrained the nation's industrial capacity.

The BTC set up a small London Plan Committee to review the proposals of the Government Committee, and this Committee delegated to a Working Party the task of preparing a detailed report, examining the planning proposals from the point of view of practical transport men.

The Working Party's report was published in the Spring of 1949. Its proposals, much more realistic than those of the Railway (London Plan) Committee, were widely discussed. A first priority scheme proposed was for a Tube from Edmonton to East Croydon, known as "Route C", which subsequently was modified to become the basis of the Victoria Line.

To sum up this period, it was a busy time, during which it was assumed that the railways would continue to form the backbone of national transport. This ignored the fact that integration had remained an elusive concept; that the nationalised Road Haulage Executive was building up a very efficient organisation which was becoming an increasingly formidable competitor; and that traders were investing heavily in road vehicles for the carriage of their own goods. Even so, railway activity between 1948 and 1953, despite some fluctuations, appeared sufficiently high to warrant moderate optimism. The index of loaded passenger train miles rose from 100 in 1948 to 104 in 1953; the index of loaded freight train miles from 100 to 105 over the same period.

The record over the period shows net traffic receipts of the passenger and freight services (excluding road collection and delivery and shipping services), before interest and central charges, as follows:

BR Surpluses

1948	£26·3m
1949	£12·7m
1950	£26·3m
1951	£35·0m
1952	£40·0m

This performance was certainly due at least in part to the economies achieved by the Railway Executive's centralised management and standardisation of practices. But had the Commission at this time allocated central charges and interest among the Executives, even on the above figures it would have been clear that the railways were failing to earn their allocated share of central charges in every year except 1952. And to have a static business within an expanding market indicates a relative decline.

The failure of the railways to make a better showing at a time when road transport was still flexing its muscles for a great post-war recovery may be attributed to three main causes:

(a) failure of the Government to make investment funds for railway modernisation available soon enough and on an adequate scale;

(b) inability of the British Transport Commission to implement the policy of integration imposed on it by the Government;

(c) the time-lag between experiencing increased costs (arising mainly from wage settlements) and authorisation by the Government to raise charges adequately to compensate for the increased costs.

The Modernisation Plan; More Power to the Regions

The Labour Government which passed the 1947 Transport Act was succeeded in 1951 by a Conservative Government which decided to amend that Act and establish an organisation more suited to its own political philosophy. Dissatisfaction by this time had become widespread with the results of the 1947 Act. All the same, both in the Railway Executive and in the Transport Commission there were certainly many younger managers who felt that a great opportunity for effectively restructuring the transport industry for the better was there, and that it would be helpful to eliminate the tension between the Commission and the Railway Executive. This had existed from the beginning and had been exacerbated by the appointment of the Members of the Railway Executive directly by the Minister of Transport, so that the Commission was unable either to choose or to change its own agents for executing its policy. The 1953 Transport Act now abolished the Executive; and, effectively, the policy of transport integration. It provided instead that the railways should be relieved of many statutory restrictions on charging, removing for instance the long-standing obligation to preserve equality between consignees of goods and to refrain from "undue preference". The scope of future Charges Schemes was to be drastically limited; the railways were now empowered to compete with road transport by quoting competitive rates within maximum levels which were the only ones that need be published.

Any lingering hope of integration was finally destroyed by the requirement in the 1953 Act that British Road Services should be denationalised. In the event, however, it proved possible only to dispose of some 24,000 out of the 40,000 vehicles of BRS; the process of denationalisation stopped, no further buyers being forthcoming, at a point which left BRS with some 16,000. Even thus reduced in size, it could be a formidable competitor of the railways.

After 1953 the railway Regions and the Commission settled down to a brief "honeymoon". The disappearance of the Railway Executive had imbued the new Regional managements with a sense of greater power and a greater say in policy. Area Boards were set up, enjoying some but not all the functions and status of the previous railway Boards of Directors, and this stimulated the feeling of independence. The Commission at first accepted this; indeed, its new Chairman, General Sir Brian (later Lord) Robertson, felt that Regional loyalties had an important part to play, on the analogy of regimental esprit de corps as an essential component in the morale of an army.

An important consequence of the transfer of control from the Railway Executive to the Commission was the immediate impetus given to accelerating the changeover from steam traction. The Regions were pressed to implement as quickly as possible the schemes for lightweight diesel trains in place of stopping steam trains in all rural (and some suburban) areas. But the desire of the Commission to carry out a wider policy of railway development was frustrated by the low levels of capital investment which the Government continued to apply. It was felt that this prevented the Commission from exploiting the potential of rail transport at a time when rapid increases were taking place both in road haulage and in "own account" road transport. Private cars were also increasing rapidly in numbers. Out of all this dissatisfaction was born, towards the end of 1954, the British Railways Plan for Modernisation and Re-Equipment, proposing a 15-year period of substantial investment.

It has since been argued by critics that the Plan came too late. This was scarcely the fault of the Commission, which year by year had argued strongly in favour of higher allocations of capital investment. It has also been said by critics that the Plan did not take sufficient account of the changed circumstances of the railways; that it assumed that they would continue to carry the same share of the nation's traffics as previously, whereas there were already signs that the railways' share of the total was declining, even though the actual levels of traffic might appear relatively static.

But the authors of the Modernisation Plan believed that, given adequate investment, the railways should be able to improve their position, both absolutely and in relative terms. The Plan itself, as published in December 1954, admitted that "British Railways today are not working at full efficiency, mainly owing to their past inability to attract enough capital investment to keep their physical equipment fully up to date". It declared that the object of the Plan was to effect a transformation of virtually all the forms of service now offered by British Railways. In particular:

(i) as regards passenger services, remodelling of the operations will provide fast, clean, regular and frequent services, electric or diesel, in all the great urban areas; inter city and main line trains will be accelerated and made more punctual; scrvices on other routes will be made reasonably economic, or will be transferred to road;

(ii) as regards freight services, there will be a complete re-orientation of operations designed to speed up movement, to reduce its cost, and to provide direct transits for main streams of traffic; and to attract to the railway a due proportion of the full-load merchandise traffic which would otherwise pass by road.

The Plan was estimated to involve an outlay of approximately £1,240m (revised in 1957 to £1,660m), over a period of about 15 years. Almost half of this, however, would be required in any case for normal maintenance of railway services over the period of the Plan.

The total economic effect of the Plan was estimated at an improvement of some £35m p.a. in passenger service receipts and £60m of freight service receipts, making £95m, from which some £10m would be deducted for increased expenses.

The Plan's main components were:

(1) Improvement of track and signalling for higher speeds, with extension of colour light signalling and automatic train control, with introduction of power-operated signal boxes and centralised traffic control where suitable.

(2) The complete replacement of steam as a form of motive power by electric or diesel traction.

(3) Replacement of locomotive-hauled passenger rolling stock by multiple-unit electric or diesel trains, and modernisation of many passenger stations and parcels depots.

(4) Major remodelling of the freight services by fitting continuous brakes to all freight wagons; replanning marshalling yards and a drastic reduction in their number; construction of larger wagons for mineral traffic.

The Plan included electrification of the existing non-electrified lines of the Southern Region east of the Reading–Portsmouth axis; of the London Tilbury & Southend line; of the Liverpool Street lines to Enfield and Chingford, Hertford and Bishops Stortford; those from King's Cross and Moorgate to Letchworth; and of the Glasgow suburban lines.

Most of these works have since been completed except for electrification of the lines from King's Cross and Moorgate which is only nearing completion at the time of writing.

The Plan also declared, however, that it was the intention to electrify two major trunk routes and one of lesser density, namely the King's Cross–Doncaster, Leeds, and York line of the Eastern Region and the Euston to Birmingham, Crewe, Liverpool, and Manchester lines of the London Midland Region; together with extension of the existing electrification from Liverpool Street as far as Ipswich, including the Clacton, Harwich, and Felixstowe branches. Of these bold projects only part has been executed.

On freight services, the Plan proposed the comprehensive rationalisation of marshalling yards, and concentration of work at a limited number of modern terminals. This was intended to reduce shunting and trip working of trains, to improve transits and concentrate sufficient tonnage at the terminals to justify capital expenditure on mechanical handling appliances.

Extremely important was the proposal to fit continuous brakes to all the wagon stock. The Plan pointed out that "Great Britain is the only major industrial nation in which a large proportion of freight traffic on the railways is still carried in loose-coupled wagons not fitted with continuous brakes. The absence of continuous brakes on freight trains necessitates slow timings and, consequently, undue occupation of the track. The additional headway required by the faster-moving trains introduces a further serious source of delay into the slower moving loose-coupled trains." Productivity of train crews would be improved by elimination of loose-coupled trains and important savings would arise from the elimination of catch points on gradients. A striking feature was an estimated saving of some 2,000 locomotives.

It has since been said that the Plan was over-ambitious in its estimate of what could be done within the programme period of 15 years, and that the technical problems were underestimated. True, certain major elements of the electrification proposals remain unfulfilled 20 years after the Plan was launched. And even today, part (though a fast-diminishing part) of the wagon fleet is still loose-coupled and fitted with handbrakes only. This is not unconnected with the decision taken in 1955 to standardise the vacuum brake, when the choice of automatic brake to be fitted to the wagon fleet was made by the Commission. The BTC's decision in favour of the vacuum brake discounted long-term advantages in favour of short-term convenience, but it has since had to be rectified.

Another criticism made of the Plan is that the policy for ordering diesel loco-motives led to a proliferation of types. The Commission here was in a dilemma; it was originally the intention to order a limited number of prototypes, and gain experience with these before deciding on a few standard types for large-scale construction. This programme was, however, accelerated because the changeover from steam to diesel traction was difficult and it was desired to obtain the bene-fits and economies from dieselisation as quickly as possible. The multiplication of types which flowed from the decision to use all available resources, whether of the private builders or BR Workshops, led to some unsuccessful designs being produced, which had to be progressively weeded out before there could be a full concentration of production upon proved and reliable machines.

The last criticism that can be made of the Modernisation Plan is that the direction of the Plan from headquarters was not sufficiently firm and that the Regions obtained too many unnecessary and sometimes capricious variations in the design of, for example, multiple-unit diesel sets and electric multiple-unit trains. But it must be remembered that over this period it was the policy of the Government, loyally carried out by the Commission, that the Regions should be given a measure of commercial and managerial freedom.

The Plan certainly produced a tonic effect overall. The warning about discarding services which could not be made economic was not taken as seriously as the forecasts of expansion. Certainly, within the Regions, the prospect of ample finance for improvements greatly stimulated the morale both of management and of the staff. But some years had to elapse before the results could show.

A feature of the Transport Act, 1947, which has already been briefly mentioned is the provision that the railways should accept a form of public accountability. The method adopted to achieve this end was the constitution of a Central Trans-port Consultative Committee and Area Transport Users' Consultative Committee. The main task of the Committees was the examination of proposals for the with-drawal of unremunerative services and the closing of unremunerative lines. The procedure in such cases was virtually that of a tribunal, with a case being pre-sented by the Commission and opposed by objectors. The effect was to apply a brake upon the closure process; even so, as early as 1955 some 130 branch line services had been withdrawn with the approval of the relevant TUCC.

The Central Transport Consultative Committee concerned itself additionally with wider questions, such as the possible use of diesel railcars; and at its request the Commission examined various propositions of this kind. The London Committee also had wider functions, having regard to the monopoly position enjoyed by London Transport and the railways jointly in the metropolitan area.

By 1955, the Commission had virtually completed the far-reaching changes in organisation which had been set in motion by the Transport Act, 1953. The new Area Boards, each controlling a Railway Region, reported direct to the Commission. Coordination of the work in the Regions thus became a task of some difficulty, and this led to the growth of a complex headquarters organisation within the Commission. At this stage the concept of a single Chief Executive controlling the railways would have been contrary to the concept of decentralisation and the intention to strengthen the functions of the Area Boards, except in so far as the Chairman of the Commission could be considered to cover this function in addition to his Chairmanship. That was certainly Sir Brian Robertson's own view.

The new organisation of the Commission was undoubtedly very complicated and criticism of it began to develop, both inside and outside the undertaking. In the end these criticisms led to the abolition of the BTC and transfer of control of the railways to the British Railways Board.

It was, ironically enough, around 1955, just when the Modernisation Plan had received official approval, that the Commission began to experience serious concern about the financial position of the railways. In their Annual Report that year, they showed an accumulated deficit of over £70m. The deterioration in the financial position continued until the end of the decade. The chief reasons for insufficient revenue were the falling-off in freight traffic and the inability to raise charges to counterbalance increased costs.

The reduction in freight traffic can be shown by the following tables:

	Net Estimated ton-miles (000m.)	Freight Receipts (£m.)
1954	22·1	273
1955	21·4	274
1956	21·5	284
1957	20·9	289
1958	18·4	259
1959	17·7	241
1960	18·7	247
1961	17·6	237

To meet this situation a radical improvement in the freight-train services was necessary if traffic was to be retained by rail. A major step was the germ of the Freightliner system which emerged during this period, with a study of the economics of larger containers than those that had hitherto been in use. Another innovation was the "merry-go-round" train, with high capacity wagons operating between collieries and power stations.

The position on the passenger side, however, was less gloomy. The figures of originating passengers were as follows:

	Passengers (m.)	Passenger-miles (m.)
1955	994	20,308
1956	1,029	21,133
1957	1,101	22,591
1958	1,090	21,725
1959	1,069	22,270
1960	1,037	21,547
1961	1,025	21,061

As wages and salaries account for over 60% of the total expenditure on the railways, the principal source of economies could only be higher productivity and a consequent substantial reduction in total staff. But the following table of staff numbers shows only a modest reduction in the eight years following the downturn in the financial position:

BR Staff Numbers

	000
end – 1954	577
1955	563
1956	571
1957	573
1958	550
1959	519
1960	515
1961	500

By the end of 1959 the Government began to doubt the financial results of modernisation and decided that individual projects should be scrutinised by Ministry of Transport officials, which had the effect of slowing down the pace. In fact, the situation finally induced a Government decision to obtain a private assessment of the organisation and efficiency of the British Transport Commission. This was entrusted to a Special Advisory Group under Sir Ivan Stedeford, which produced several reports to the Minister of Transport on aspects of the Commission's organisation and operations. At the same time, as part of its normal function, the Parliamentary Select Committee on Nationalised Industries turned its attention to the railways. Its Report was not published until July 1960 and was partially reassuring.

However, the views of Sir Ivan Stedeford and his Special Advisory Group, though they were not published, were more critical. They persuaded the Government that major changes were required. The first was to disband the British Transport Commission. The principal purpose of the Commission, to integrate all public inland transport, had disappeared; it could now be argued that any necessary co-ordination could be entrusted to the Ministry of Transport. And as an organisation for business management, the Commission was considered top-heavy and complicated.

The second charge was to be in motivation. The railways in future were to be run less as an essential public service, more as a competitive enterprise that must refrain from looking to the public purse for subsidy and must show that future investment in it could be justified by normal financial criteria.

Though this period closed with expressions of Government dissatisfaction with the BTC, it should not be forgotten that during it some quite substantial technical advances were made. Most of the fruits of the Modernisation Plan were not apparent until the 1960s, although the modern image of British Rail is derived largely from the initial work done under the Plan. Projection of the new image started when a Railway Design Panel was set up in 1956, "to advise on the best means of obtaining a high standard of appearance and amenity in the design of its equipment". A strong corporate identity for British railways as a whole was overdue. The Railway Executive in 1948 had tried out a number of experimental liveries and eventually evolved a standard of "maroon-and-cream" for main-line stock, and plain "maroon" for non-compartment vehicles, with Southern Region green for electric multiple-unit trains. Most locomotives were painted black; express passenger types only, dark green.

During the period of decentralisation some latitude was given by the BTC to painting named trains in Regional colours. Other stock displayed a standard livery based on LMS red, except on the Southern Region. But the impossibility of keeping vehicles painted, for instance in GWR chocolate-and-cream, to fixed rosters led to a somewhat piebald appearance of trains on occasion, and the tentative move towards Regional colours was discontinued.

Eventually, out of separate studies for the Glasgow suburban electric scheme, for uniforms and for station signposting, the project of an all-embracing BR house style was evolved, agreed by the Board and launched in 1965. The abbreviated name British Rail was adopted, together with the now familiar two-way arrow symbol, and the standard "Rail Blue" livery. This was gradually introduced for all locomotives and carriages, with grey upper panels for main-line stock. Distinctive lettering was adopted for all signs and printed material. New, more modern uniforms too were eventually issued in 1966. After some initial doubts, they were accepted as being smarter as well as more practical by the staff and the public.

Re-shaping in the Beeching Era

Dr Richard Beeching (later Lord Beeching) who at the time was Technical Director of ICI and had been an active member of the Stedeford Advisory Group, was appointed Chairman of the BTC on 1 June 1961, succeeding Lord (formerly Sir Brian) Robertson. He immediately inaugurated a process of simplifying the organisation, whilst the Government introduced a new Transport Bill which, when it became the Transport Act, 1962, abolished the BTC and placed the railways under a new British Railways Board, of which Dr Beeching was appointed Chairman as from 1 January 1963. The Act drastically reduced the capital liabilities of the railways, the principle being to write off the assets prior to the modernisation outlays, in the hope of establishing a firm basis for a purely commercial policy.

The Area Boards were replaced by Regional Boards of which, in most cases, the Regional General Managers became Chairmen. This provided a simpler and quicker chain of command; but co-ordination of functions at headquarters presented problems that often needed to be settled by the Chairman himself.

Under Dr Beeching's inspiration, a major study of the railways' commercial and financial activities was launched, with the object of drafting a policy under which the railways (in whatever form they might continue) would no longer require a subsidy from public funds. This study took shape in two major reports called, respectively, The Re-Shaping of British Railways and The Development of the Major Trunk Routes.

The "Re-Shaping" Report of 1963 has been well described as "the full catalogue of the industry's problems". The chief legitimate criticism that can be levied at the Report is that it should, logically, have preceded and not followed the Modernisation Plan of 1954: but that was not the fault of its authors. The Report was a deep and in many ways constructive analysis of the problems of the railways in the post-war world. It agreed that it is "the responsibility of the British Railways Board so to shape and operate the railways as to make them pay"; but this was qualified by a clear statement that "the proposals now made are not directed towards achieving that result by the simple and unsatisfactory method of rejecting all those parts of the system which do not pay already or which cannot be made to pay easily. On the contrary, the changes proposed are intended to shape the railways to meet present-day requirements by enabling them to provide as much of the total transport of the country as they can provide well".

Moreover, the Report did not ignore social benefit; it suggested clearly that "it might pay to run railways at a loss in order to prevent the incidence of an even greater cost which would arise elsewhere if the railways were closed".

This constructive approach was, however, followed by some startling figures obtained from an analysis of the route system and from surveys of traffic. It appeared that one-third of the route mileage carried only 1% of the passenger-miles; in freight, the traffic position was equally astonishing, since one-half of the mileage carried only about 5% of the total freight ton-miles.

The figures for stations were as surprising as those for the routes. One-half of the passenger stations produced less than 2% of the total passenger receipts; at the other end of the scale, 34 stations, or less than 1% of the total, produced 26% of the receipts. Of the freight stations, one-half produced less than 3% of the station freight receipts.

The Report dealt also with utilisation of rolling-stock and pointed out that some 2,000 main-line coaches, kept in reserve for peak traffics, were only required on 10 occasions in the year on average; another 4,000 were required on only 18 occasions or less.

The Report's Appendices, setting out proposals for closure of lines and stations, produced considerable public alarm. They suggested, on the economic tests applied in the Report, withdrawal of some 245 passenger train services, and closure of over 2,000 passenger stations, in addition to those which were already under consideration for closure at the time of publication of the Report.

Implementation of the Report was by no means as rapid as its authors may have hoped and expected. This was partly because of the procedure whereby closures had to be submitted to the appropriate Transport Users' Consultative Committee, partly because of the political implications of such a dramatic scaling-down of the system, on which (naturally enough) the railway Unions expressed strong views. The actual trend of line closures between 1962 and 1969 was:

	BR Route-Miles Open for Traffic (nearest 00)
end – 1962	17,500
1963	17,000
1964	16,000
1965	14,900
1966	13,700
1967	13,200
1968	12,400
1969	12,100

But it must again be stressed that the "Re-shaping" Report was not dominated by the need to withdraw services and close stations. It was constructive as well. For example, in an important Appendix it described fully the "Liner Train" concept (later to develop into Freightliner).

The Development of the Major Trunk Routes, published in February 1965, began by saying that it was regrettable, although perhaps not surprising, that public attention had concentrated upon the proposed abandonment of the financially unsound parts of the railway system. Constructive proposals for the development of a new railway were much more important. The Report then analysed the present pattern of traffic between main centres of population and industry, the changes in the economy likely to affect transport over the next 20 years, and the expected pattern of transport demand between main centres in 1984.

Taking all these factors into account, certain trunk routes were nominated as suitable for carrying the expected traffic flows, converted into train loads. In many cases it was found that duplicate routes existed and that, by concentration of major flows upon one route, very substantial economies could be obtained.

As in the case of the "Re-shaping" proposals, however, the action taken following the Report fell short of what had been proposed. For instance, the East Coast route to Edinburgh still retains most of its former importance, affected only to a minor extent by the Euston–Glasgow electrification. The Settle and Carlisle route remains in being, though primarily for freight.

On the other hand, the Great Central line to London has been closed. There has been a concentration where services formerly were duplicated, for example, London–Leeds is now based on King's Cross; London–Sheffield on St Pancras; London–Exeter on Paddington. Former main lines such as Salisbury–Exeter, Ipswich–Yarmouth, Oxford–Worcester, and Sheffield (Victoria)–Manchester, have been downgraded, and sometimes reduced from two tracks to a single line. More intensive working of rolling-stock, with quick turnrounds at terminal stations, has greatly improved the economics and thereby helped to ensure the future of the main network.

Despite these quite strenuous measures, which led to a progressive reduction in staff numbers from 475,000 at end-1962 to 269,000 at end-1968, the deficit continued, the figures (after interest charges) being

BR Deficits

	£m.
1962	159
1963	137
1964	125
1965	137
1966	136
1967	156
1968	151

Yet even though "business" management did not transform the economic situation of the railways to the hoped-for extent, during the period a number of major developments emerged which closely affect the character of British Rail today. Some of course took some time to come to fruition, but nearly all have their roots in this period of change and challenge.

See Plate 57

One of the first developments, at the beginning of the decade, was the introduction of the "Blue Pullmans" between London and Manchester and London and Bristol. Associated improvements in passenger comfort included the development of better bogies, the introduction of long-welded rails, and the widespread increase in speeds which followed the introduction of the "Deltic" diesel locomotives of 3,300 h.p. on the Great Northern main line.

See Plate 68

In 1962 several of the electrification schemes under the Modernisation Plan were completed, including the Southern Region electrification to Folkestone, Dover and Ramsgate via Ashford, and the London–Tilbury–Southend line. The first prototype Mark II coaching vehicle also appeared in this year, and in 1965 the first Freightliner service between London and Glasgow was opened. In 1967 the Southern Region electrification to Southampton and Bournemouth was completed.

A system of automatic warning control, representing a major development of the systems of automatic train control used on the former Great Western Railway and on part of the former LMS Railway, was standardised for gradual introduction on all main lines.

See Plate 66

On the freight side, the concept of complete "customer trains" of special-purpose wagons for single traffics was developed. The oil companies were persuaded to use rail, and large bogie tank wagons began to appear.

But perhaps the most important single advance was the opening of the London Midland Region electrification from London to Liverpool and Manchester in 1966, following which, and crowning the work of the decade, in 1968 HM The Queen opened the new Euston Station.

See Plate 78

Reference has already been made to the post-war completion of the electrification schemes in the 1935–40 New Works Programme, which included Tube extensions and projection of Underground trains over various British Railways suburban lines in Greater London. Thereafter the only comparable new work for some time was the electrification from Rickmansworth to Amersham and Chesham, opened in 1960, and the four-tracking, Harrow-on-the-Hill to Watford South Junction, completed in 1962.

Meanwhile, a long campaign was conducted by London Transport, supported by the British Transport Commission, to persuade the Government to authorise the construction of Route "C" of the London Plan Working Party, re-christened the Victoria Line in 1955. Eventually, after much pressure and an independent cost/benefit study of the new Tube's justification, it was authorised in 1962, and initially opened in three stages from Walthamstow Central to Highbury, and later to Warren Street, in 1968. The section from Warren Street to Victoria was ceremonially opened by HM The Queen in March 1969, the extension to Brixton, $3\frac{1}{2}$ miles long, following in 1971.

A Fresh Start

It was inevitable that the Labour Government which came to office in 1964 would disagree with the principle of treating British Railways as a purely commercial undertaking, and it became clear from the discussions which took place between the Board and the Government that radical changes in policy were intended. Dr Beeching retired from the Chairmanship on 1 June 1965 and was succeeded by Mr (later Sir Stanley) Raymond, who relinquished his appointment as Chairman on 31 December 1967, being succeeded by Mr H. C. (later Sir Henry) Johnson. Sir Henry Johnson retired on 11 September 1971, and was succeeded by the Rt. Hon. Richard Marsh, who had been a Member and Joint Deputy Chairman of the Board since 3 May 1971.

A great deal of thought was being given by the Government to the problems of nationalised transport. In a White Paper, "Transport Policy", published in

July 1966, it was stated that four basic themes were shaping its transport policy. These were:

1. That transport infrastructure and services must be modernised, with overall planning of investment;
2. Traffic in towns must be dealt with by integrated planning in the big conurbations;
3. Social as well as economic criteria must be taken into account;
4. Public road and rail services must be integrated on a functional basis.

The problems of the railways were studied in detail by a Joint Steering Group appointed by the Ministry of Transport and the Chairman of the British Railways Board, which reported in 1967. The main proposals of the Group were embodied in the Transport Act, 1968.

When the Bill appeared it was clear that the Government had accepted the important new principle that the "commercial" system should be separated from the "social" services. This, however, applied only on the passenger side; the entire freight services were expected to be run on commercial lines. The "commercial" passenger services were intended to be fully viable, but the Government would support the "social" services by means of specific grants for individual services. This involved an analysis which was not always easy to carry out, particularly in the London area, where a single block grant for commuter and other social services had to be made. Henceforth the Government would announce annually the level of grant-aid for the maintenance of passenger services, the object being to run the total down progressively, year by year. Each individual closure, however, was still open to scrutiny under the consultative procedure.

On the freight side, where services were much more difficult to dissect and cost accurately, a quite different form of surgery was to be undertaken. The largest single loss-maker identified in the "Re-shaping" Report had been the Sundries business of small consignments by rail, involving road collection and delivery. It was decided to set up a separate, specialised organisation, National Carriers Ltd, a subsidiary of the National Freight Corporation, which also controlled British Road Services, to take over this business. Rail would be employed where loads could be bulked and transferred to rail for economical trunk hauls. More questionable perhaps was the decision to remove control of the Liner Train business from the railways and hand it over to a separate Freightliner Company in which the British Railways Board would only hold a minority interest.

A major effect of the Act on the railway freight business was that the railway motor vehicles and the freight terminals handling sundries traffic were transferred to National Carriers Ltd.

Although the Transport Act, 1968, did not provide for integration of passenger services nationally, it did establish a form of local integration. In major conurbations (initially the West Midlands, Merseyside, Greater Manchester and Tyneside) a Passenger Transport Authority was set up, under which a Passenger Transport

Executive would undertake the managerial work. So far as the railways were concerned, it was provided that the Executives would enter into agreements with them for the running of suburban railway services, the fares to be charged and any subsidy required for the maintenance of those that were uneconomic. In other words, commuter railway services in these conurbations might if necessary be supported from the proceeds of local rates.

The consequence of the 1968 Act was a slowing down in the rate of reduction of the route mileage, as shown by the following table:

BR Route Miles Open	(nearest 00)
end – 1963	17,000
1967	13,200
1971	11,600
1972	11,400
1973	11,300

The 1968 Act also assisted the railway finances by cancelling much of the outstanding capital debt, the remaining debt being regarded as the "live" capital upon which the railways might reasonably be expected to earn a normal rate of return. For the first two years after the Act came into operation, the Board did in fact earn a small surplus. In 1969 it was £15m. after interest charges; in 1970 it was £9·5m.

During the first half of the 1970s, development continued. In 1971, the Government gave approval to electrification of the Great Northern Suburban Lines from King's Cross. In 1972, the prototype "PEP" suburban train, of a design totally different from any previously operated on the Southern Region, began trials; in 1973 the first Mark III coaching vehicles began to appear in prototype form. But the most important development of 1974 was undoubtedly the extension of electrification from Weaver Junction to Glasgow, thus inaugurating the first all-electric Anglo-Scottish route.

During the period there was also close collaboration between BR and the Passenger Transport Executives established under the 1968 Act, leading to several important rail development schemes being jointly planned, including the Mersey Rail Link and the "Pic-Vic" tunnel in Manchester. Another important development was the intensive planning which British Rail embarked upon, in very close association with the French Railways, covering all the rail aspects of the Channel Tunnel project.

In 1971 a project was initiated to provide continuous monitoring of freight movements, with the location of individual wagons and their contents being instantly ascertainable. This involved the adoption of a fully computerised "real time" freight information and transit control system known shortly as TOPS (Total Operations Processing System). TOPS enables freight traffic to be monitored and controlled with a precision hitherto unknown in railway operation. Its installation was phased over the years 1973–5.

Looking at the freight business in its entirety, between 1965 and 1975 its characteristics changed significantly. This was mainly because of the decline in the use of coal, traditionally the principal bulk traffic handled by the railways. In the place of coal, a growing volume of other bulk traffics arose, such as petroleum, building materials and cars. Much of this was between customer-owned terminals. There was an increase overall in train-load traffic from 62m. tons to 135m. tons between 1967 and 1973. The emphasis on train-load traffic led to a reduction in the total number of freight terminals from some 4,900 at the end of 1967 to about 2,700 at the end of 1973.

The effect of these changes was a reduction in the total wagon fleet from 470,000 in 1967 to about 250,000. There has been a progressive replacement of the smaller general-purpose wagons by modern high-capacity wagons, frequently designed to carry one specific traffic.

In the 1968 Transport Act, the British Railways Board had been required to undertake a review of the affairs of the Board "for the purpose of determining whether the carrying on of their activities is organised . . . in the most efficient manner and to report their conclusions to the Minister". The Board accordingly proposed to assume to itself a mainly non-executive role, and "give greater emphasis to overall corporate planning, policy-making and longer-term direction of British Rail and each of its other businesses, whilst ensuring that each business is effectively managed". Subsidiary boards were to be set up for each of the businesses other than railways. In each business a Chief Executive would be appointed, including one for the railways. The outline proposals of the report were approved by the Minister in 1969, and the new organisation that took shape in 1970 followed them fairly closely.

The Board followed this internal reorganisation at top level by a study of the "Field" Organisation, covering all levels of management, including the Regions, Divisions and Area/Stations/Depots. A report entitled *Re-structuring the Railway Field Organisation* was completed in January 1971 and was accepted by the Board, subject to the development of a detailed implementation plan. The main features of the Plan were the replacement of Regions by a larger number of smaller "Territories" and the shortening of the chain of command by replacing Regions, Divisions and Areas by Territories and Areas. Eventually eight territories were designated and preparations for the gradual changeover were put in hand. The Field Organisation also involved a substantial transfer of all the planning functions and the determination of commercial and technical policy from the Regions to BRB Headquarters. Territory headquarters were to be established as far as possible in provincial locations, each representing a natural "centre of gravity" of the territory. Implementation of the proposals proved to be a complex task, involving prolonged consultations with the staff, and Trade Union objections halted the project at the end of 1974.

Unfortunately, the 1968 Act, despite the capital reconstruction and the grant-aid provision for unremunerative "social" services, did not provide a lasting solution to the financial problem. The tide again turned and in 1971 the deficit was £15·4m; in 1972, £26·2m, and in 1973, £51·6m. (In each year there was a profit on operating account, turned into a deficit after interest and other financial charges.) The position was eased in 1973 by special non-recurring grants from the Government totalling £72m. to meet the cash-flow shortfall. But this was obviously only a palliative; and already by June 1972 a full review of the railways' position and prospects had been called for by the Minister for Transport Industries.

The Board submitted its review in June 1973. The Minister had asked it to consider three questions. What had gone wrong in the past? Is there a viable railway network? Is there a "necessary" railway network? The Board explained the problems that it had faced since nationalisation, the effects of the enormous expansion in car ownership and in road haulage, of the decline in coal consumption and of the recurring slumps in the iron and steel industry. It emphasised the achievements in face of these difficulties, in providing improved services and higher productivity. It did not consider that any substantially smaller network would be financially viable; and the costs of scaling down (such as redundancy payments to staff) would be substantial. Nor could it define a "necessary railway"; this could only be done as a part of national transport policy, which it was for the Government to define.

The review then gave forecasts of growth over the next ten years in the passenger business, mainly in the Inter-City sector, in Freightliner, and other train-load freight. However, a decline was expected in wagon-load freight. Greater efficiency would reduce the number of locomotives, carriages and wagons in use, and staff numbers would fall by about 2% p.a.

This programme was estimated to require a total investment over the ten years of £1,787m. On 28 November 1973 the Minister of Transport Industries said in the House of Commons that the Government had accepted the Board's views in general. Whilst investment would not be quite at the level desired by the Board, the system would be maintained at approximately its present size.

The Act also reduced the capital debt of the British Railways Board from £439m. to £250m., thereby reducing interest charges by about £40m. p.a. It authorised increased borrowing by the Board and did away with the specific grants for individual unremunerative passenger services authorised by the 1968 Act. Instead, it allowed the Secretary of State to give general directions to the BRB about the operation of passenger services and to make compensation payments (up to a possible total of £1,500m.) to enable the railways to carry out these general directions. In return, the railways would have to consult the Government more closely in developing their policies, especially on the five-year "rolling" corporate plans. A major departure from the principle of the 1968 Act was the provision that Government grants might be made available to assist the provision of rail freight terminal facilities.

On the face of it, this should give the railways some measure of security in planning for the future. But the railways have, as these pages have shown, encountered many changes, sometimes abrupt, in Government policy. Although they

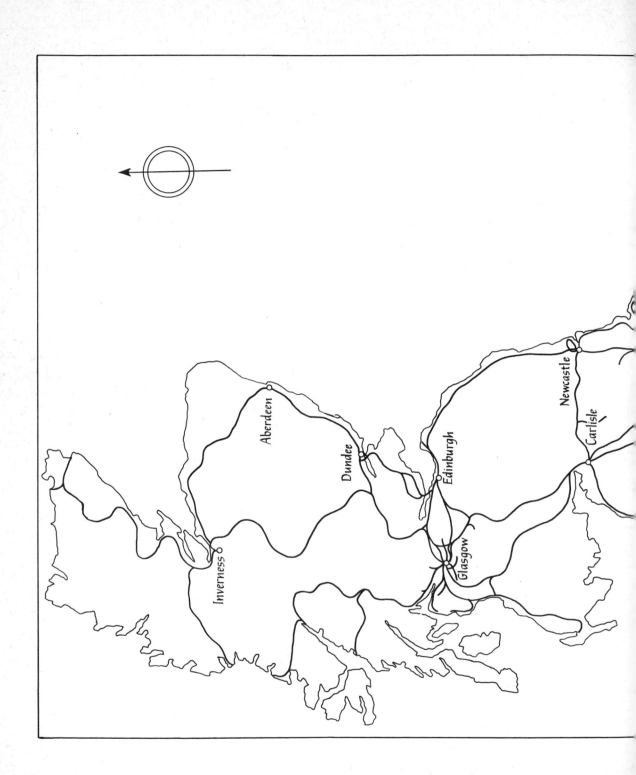

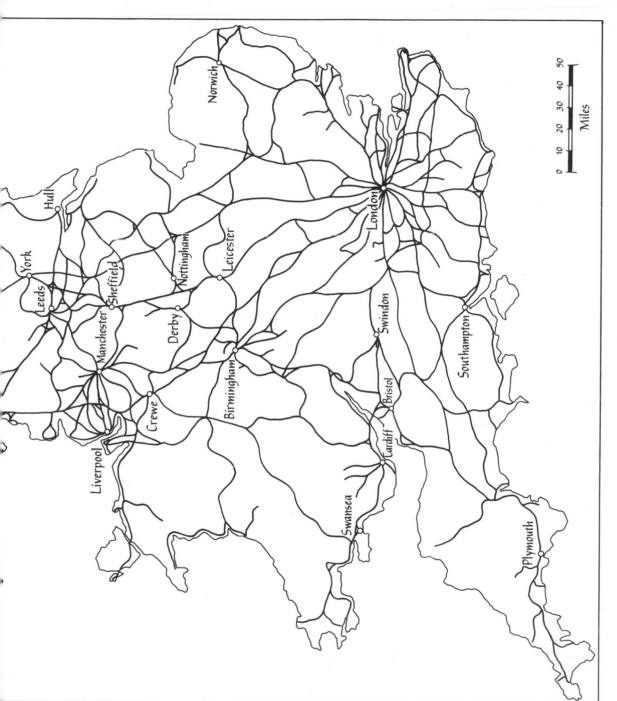

5   The British Railway system in 1975

have survived, their ability to provide the best possible service to the community
has often suffered.

The "Other Businesses"

The four main-line Companies which were nationalised on 1 January 1948 were
more than purely railway undertakings. The "non-railway" businesses that came
under the control of the British Railways Board created in 1962 comprised the
hotels, refreshment rooms and restaurant cars; the shipping services and packet
ports; workshops; property; and a research organisation. The road vehicle fleet
of collection and delivery vehicles remained under railway control until the
Transport Act, 1968, transferred them to the National Freight Corporation.

British Transport Hotels Ltd is a subsidiary Company of the Board, succeeding
the Hotels and Catering Services Division of the BTC and the earlier Hotels
Executive. Nationalisation of the railways brought together under one management for the first time all the hotels of the former railway Companies. They were
an assortment of varying standards, the result of differing management policies.
A review of their profitability and prospects was put in hand and the foundations
were laid of a programme of modernisation, improvement and rationalisation
based on retention of the best. In some cities it was felt that there was scope for
two hotels, of rather different character, as for example in Glasgow, where the
Central and North British Hotels were maintained. Some resort hotels which were
not considered to have a successful future, such as the Felix Hotel at Felixstowe,
were sold. Unfortunately, restrictions on capital investment, applied first to the
British Transport Commission and later to the British Railways Board, prevented
any very substantial investment in new buildings or complete rebuilding, a
notable exception being the construction of the Old Course Hotel at St Andrews
in 1968. But between the late 1960s and 1975 some £8m. was spent on improvements, extensions, bathroom schemes, new bars, restaurants, kitchens and saunas.

See Plate 60 Refreshment rooms have never been as profitable as the hotels, but they were
and are an essential adjunct to rail travel. Accordingly a policy of modernising
the rooms and of introducing a more varied range of food and drink was pursued.
It was greatly speeded up in 1970 when a £5m. five-year programme of refurbish-
ing was begun. In recent years, moreover, a policy of giving selected station
restaurants a distinctive character or "theme" of their own was adopted.

Restaurant-car catering has its special problems, such as the restricted size of
kitchens, difficulty in arranging suitable working circuits both to suit the needs
of travellers and to enable the staff to work reasonable hours, and the need to
provide supplies at strategic points. Even so, since nationalisation there has been
a steady growth in the number of restaurant-car services on BR, which rose to 900
See Plate 59 daily by 1975. In pre-war days, the traditional "dining car" offered a substantial
table d'hôte meal at a very reasonable price. During the war the range of meals
necessarily had to be severely curtailed, and the post-war disappearance of food
rationing was a slow process. It became clear that train catering would have to be

modified. On the principal trains, a kitchen/buffet car was coupled to an open saloon, in which set meals could be provided, the buffet end of the car providing snacks and drinks. The marshalling of the train was generally such that the first-class accommodation was adjacent to the dining vehicle, the second-class accommodation being next to the buffet end of the kitchen/buffet car.

A simple type of buffet car, generally staffed by a crew of two, is provided on other services, such as the Waterloo–Portsmouth line, whilst the "miniature buffet", staffed by one man, provides an even simpler but still effective service on certain trains, for example, the Eastern Region Cambridge line.

Some of the pre-nationalisation Companies had entrusted catering services to the Pullman Car Company. The LNER had had several all-Pullman trains. The Southern Railway had had a few all-Pullman trains, but for the most part a single Pullman car, for first-class passengers only, was provided in services on the Central Division and also on Continental boat trains. After nationalisation, the contracts with the Pullman Car Company were transferred to British Railways. Later, owing to the high cost of replacing the Pullman cars (and a certain amount of pressure from the railway Unions), the Pullman services were gradually integrated with those of British Railways.

On 1 January 1948 the BTC acquired 122 ships and vessels totalling over 60,000 net registered tons. Amongst major developments since then, perhaps the most important have been the growth in car ferry services for motorists and roll-on/roll-off freight for international road transport; and the provision of container ships between Britain and the Continent and also Ireland.

See Plate 74

Ships have of course increased very considerably in size: the largest ships in the service of British Railways at nationalisation were the *Cambria* and *Hibernia* of 2,722 net registered tons; the largest ship today is the *St Edmund* of 4,697 net registered tons. Propulsion has changed from the basic oil-fired steam turbine vessel to the diesel-engined motor vessel. The "classic" passenger ship, catering mainly for passengers making train journeys on either side of the sea passage, has been replaced by the all-purpose ship, which is both a car ferry and a roll-on/roll-off carrier, and has accommodation for classic passengers in addition. In some cases this type of vessel serves three purposes, also being a train ferry. Development of the packet ports has matched the expansion of this fleet and the change in the nature of the traffic. The new car ferry dock at Folkestone and the new terminal at Parkeston Quay are striking examples.

The shipping fleets of the various railway Companies, which for many years continued to be operated by the railway Regions, were unified in 1969 when central management was introduced, leading to the creation of the Shipping & International Services Division of the British Railways Board. This in turn led to entry of the BR shipping services into a partnership with its Continental associates in France, Belgium, and Holland under the trading name of "Sealink".

See Plate 75

In 1966 it was decided by the British Railways Board to exploit the advantages of hovercraft, initially for the services in the sheltered waters between Southampton and Cowes. Later, hovercraft services were introduced with much larger craft between Dover and Boulogne/Calais. The hovercraft services have maintained a service even in weather which originally was considered quite unsuitable for this type of craft and now provide a useful complement to the services by conventional ships.

On nationalisation, the British Transport Commission inherited from the railway Companies a substantial landed estate, with the consequent need of an extensive Estate Surveyor's Department to manage it. The work of this Department markedly increased between 1948 and 1975.

The upsurge in property development which has been a feature of the last twenty years led the railways to seek to exploit the potential of the many sites they owned, particularly railway stations in city centres. Railway Sites Ltd was set up in September 1961 to form associations with developers and to progress major schemes. The work of this Company was transferred in 1965 to the Property Committee of the BRB and subsequently in 1969 to a British Rail Property Board, set up to control all property matters for all the BR Board's undertakings

The Board participated in many successful ventures with developers, which included estate developments as well as reconstructed stations in London (Cannon Street and Holborn Viaduct), at Barking, Birmingham (New Street), Crawley, Harrogate, Southampton, and Southport. Measured against the successes were a number of disappointments, partly resulting from building cost increases, partly from restrictive planning policy.

Before nationalisation, only limited research was carried out by the main-line Companies, although the LMS Railway had pioneered its own centre at Derby. This undertook much more than the routine testing of materials, which was carried out in the laboratories attached to the other railway Companies' engineering departments. The BTC however appointed a Chief Research Officer in 1949 to co-ordinate all aspects of research throughout the undertaking. But the existence of the Executives was not conducive to the centralisation of research, which continued rather slowly and spasmodically until after their disappearance.

See Plate 77   A major step forward was the decision taken in 1962 to set up a central research establishment at Derby, adjacent to the large construction workshops that had existed there for many years. The Engineering Division of the Research Department moved into these new laboratories when they were opened by HRH the Duke of Edinburgh in 1964. These laboratories, with later additions, provide unique facilities for research.

The pre-nationalisation railway Companies (unlike the railways in most parts of the world) all maintained very extensive workshops for the building as well as the repair of locomotives, carriages, and wagons. This continued after nationalisation with the shops for a time being still under Regional control. In 1962, however, the responsibility for the works was transferred from the Chief Mechanical and Electrical Engineers of the Regions in which they were situated to a separate Workshops Division of the British Transport Commission.

Shortly afterwards the "Workshop Plan" of 1962 laid down a five-year programme for the closure of 15 of the 31 main workshops; the modernisation and re-equipment of the remaining 16 at a cost of £17 million; and the rationalisation of activities at the retained works. This programme was virtually complete by the end of 1967, but by 1975 the number of main works had been further reduced to 13.

The decision by the British Railways Board to form a wholly-owned subsidiary Company to control these works followed the Transport Act of 1968, which allowed the railway works to manufacture rolling-stock and general engineering products for private customers, in addition to their primary role of providing a construction and repair service to British Rail. British Rail Engineering Ltd came into being in January 1970. It was one of the largest engineering concerns in the country and, after success in securing outside contracts, assumed a place amongst the world's leading rolling-stock builders.

Retrospect

Some nationalised industries have to work within markets which are tending to contract, owing to economic forces and changing technology. Others, more fortunate, operate in markets which are expanding. In the quarter-century and more during which British Railways have been nationalised, railways throughout the world have been generally contracting in the face of road and air competition.

In Britain, the railways have suffered largely because of the absence of any single continuing objective set them by successive Governments. Each of a series of Transport Acts has created a major upheaval in the industry, requiring time for implementation. But not enough time has been allowed before a new Act has reversed the policy of its predecessor.

Against this background of changing objectives and organisations imposed from outside, some striking achievements must be recorded. The Inter-City passenger services, the Freightliner network, the Red Star Parcels service, the Company trains for large users of rail freight – these are all success stories. There is, however, a mixture of old and new, of satisfactory and less satisfactory performance, that is difficult to sum up in a phrase. Only those with long experience of the industry will know how difficult of achievement have been the successes; how understandable, in terms of human nature, the shortcomings.

It remains the fact that the British taxpayer enjoys an Inter-City express train service that is more frequent and regular than any other in Europe, a London suburban service of unparallelled density, a unique Freightliner network, and rail catering on a much higher proportion of the trains than anywhere else. And he provides for his railways a smaller subsidy than in most large countries of Europe.

51 BR standard "Britannia" class Pacific locomotive 70028 *Royal Star* on the up Capitals United Express (Cardiff–London) near Twyford.

52 The nationalised railways made a number of experiments with alternatives to steam traction. Here is a gas-turbine locomotive tried on the Western Region from 1952 onwards. Though it developed greater power than any locomotive previously used in Britain, it was not a success in service and was soon withdrawn.

53 Lightweight diesel multiple-unit trains were introduced from 1954 onwards. Here is one crossing the Forth Bridge on its way from Edinburgh to Dundee.

54 Electric multiple-unit train, introduced on the Glasgow suburban services in 1960.

55 Electric multiple-unit express train for the London–Bournemouth service, converted from steam traction in 1967.

56 Bristol–London express headed by diesel locomotive, class 47, running beside the Avon shortly after leaving Bristol.

57　The latest type of BR electric locomotive, class 87, at work on the main West Coast line.

58　The experimental Advanced Passenger Train on its test track in Nottinghamshire.

59   Restaurant car (air-conditioned Mark III stock).

60   The Drum cafeteria at Waterloo station, opened in 1972.

61   A commuters' station rebuilt: Maze Hill (London S.E.).

62   A country station rebuilt: Wool (Dorset).

63   Motorail service carrying passengers and their cars, on the main line between Newton Abbot and Plymouth.

64　Train of 2-tier "Cartic" wagons.

65　Train of containers belonging to the Ford Motor Co. *en route* from its Merseyside factory to Harwich for transshipment to a Freightliner ship (Plate 76).

66 Gulf Oil train preparing to leave Milford Haven, S. Wales.

67 Freightliner train, electrically hauled along the West Coast main line.

68 Laying long-welded track: a photograph taken in earlier days, before the wearing of the orange-coloured "high visibility vests" had been made compulsory.

69 The platelayer gives place today to the machine: mechanised track maintenance equipment.

70 Modern colour-light signalling. Saltley power signal-box near Birmingham, which, with two others at Trent and Derby, controls 242 route miles of line, replacing 180 signal-boxes of the old type.

71 The power signal-box at Bristol, controlling 114 route miles.

72 Power signal-box at Paisley.

73 Train on the Victoria Line, the first section of which was opened in 1968. The driving is largely automatic (see p. 187).

74 Car ferry *Hengist* operating on the short sea crossing from Dover.

75   Hovercraft *The Princess Margaret* operating between Dover and Boulogne.

76   Container ship in service between Harwich and the Netherlands.

77 British Rail Research Centre at Derby: Brunel House (at the top) under construction.

78 The new Euston station. Robert Stephenson, engineer of the line from London to Birmingham, looks down on the forecourt.

4. Today and Tomorrow

The autumn of 1973 marked a turning-point in British Rail's fortunes, and with it a fundamental change in the attitude of both Government and public opinion about the role railways should play in the economy. There were two elements in it. One was a conscious decision by the Government that BR should no longer be judged by purely commercial criteria – the black-and-white judgment of profitability – and the other a matter of chance: the oil crisis precipitated by the decision of the Middle-Eastern oil-producing nations to quadruple prices and restrict production. Overnight the economies of the western world were disrupted by the end of what had been taken for granted for half a century: an unlimited supply of cheap oil and petrol. It shattered a faith that had dominated economists, town-planners and governments in Britain and the rest of the world in the post-war years. Not only were the economics of transport dramatically changed but, perhaps more important, the nation suddenly became aware of the need for a system of transport that was largely independent of the vagaries of Middle-East oil potentates or, where relying on diesel traction, was a great deal more economic in the use of an increasingly expensive and possibly scarce fuel.

It coincided, too, with a significant change in public opinion, a change summed up in the phrase "the environmentalist lobby"; a vocal and increasingly well-organised grouping of many different people and interests concerned about the pollution of the atmosphere by petrol fumes, in revolt against the ravaging of the countryside by the apparently inexorable advance of the motorway, angered by the damage done to towns and villages, infuriated by the traffic congestion that was gradually strangling movement and civilised life in London and other towns. The public no longer believed in, nor could the nation afford, the motorised dream.

This, then, was the social and economic background against which John Peyton, the Minister for Transport Industries, announced the Government's conclusions about BR's future in a policy statement in the House of Commons in November 1973, the result of a detailed analysis of the economics and future role of the railways which he had initiated on taking office after the Conservative Government came to power in 1970.

The Conservative victory and Peyton's appointment had been greeted with apprehension by the BR Board and those concerned with the future of the railways. The Conservative Party had very close links with, and financial support from, the road-haulage industry; it was passionately opposed to nationalisation, and BR, as the most exposed of the nationalised industries, had long been the Aunt Sally for politicians anxious to prove that nationalisation was synonymous with incompetence and inefficiency; a costly burden on the taxpayer which an earlier Conservative Government had given Dr (later Lord) Beeching the task of cutting down to size and making profitable. He had succeeded in the first of these objectives; BR's network in 1973 was 11,500 miles, compared with 15,000 in 1962 when the Doctor got to work, but the goal of profitability was no nearer realisation a decade later.

Peyton had a long and established reputation as a critic of nationalisation in general, and of British Rail in particular, and he was a dedicated advocate of the current ethos in the Conservative Party that rejected any form of State aid to industry; "lame ducks", it was argued, must stand on their own feet – make a profit or disappear – and BR, with its lamentable financial record, stood high in the list of "lame ducks". Peyton drove the point home at one of his first meetings with the Board when he put them the simple blunt question: "When are you going to get off the taxpayer's back?"

His crusading zeal found eager support from the Treasury, which wanted to be rid of the budgetary burden of supporting BR, and also from the powerful road lobby and among senior officials in his own Department who, in keeping with the fashionable trends of the 1960s, saw the solution to the nation's transport problems in a fresh dose of Dr Beeching's medicine, combined with ever faster building of motorways – not only on the main arterial routes but even for commuter traffic into London. The one million who flood into and out of the metropolis each day could, it was argued, be carried more cheaply by an endless flow of buses running on multi-lane urban motorways.

The review which Peyton ordered turned out to be the most detailed and thorough investigation of the economics of rail transport ever carried out in Britain or indeed in any other country. The result of the Railways Board's labours emerged in the "Red Book", a 90-page analysis of all the possible variations open to the Government, ranging from keeping the existing system open and supported by the State to the ultimate extreme of a total closure. It started with the blunt – and long overdue – recognition that the Board was losing money, would continue to do so and could therefore not meet the financial obligations laid down by Parliament in the 1968 Transport Act and all earlier railway legislation: namely to operate, at a profit, a commercial system in competition with alternative road and air transport. From this point it posed these questions:

1. What lessons can be learnt from previous attempts to "put the railways on a sound basis"?
2. What is the viable railway: i.e., one that can be made profitable?
3. What is the necessary railway: i.e., a system that meets the social and economic needs of the nation and does so at the minimum cost to the user and the taxpayer?
4. These questions involve making a judgment of the comparative position and contribution to the economy of railways and roads, the cost of maintaining a railway network compared with the building and maintenance of motorways and roads, together with all the other ancillary services provided by the state for the road user such as policing and traffic control.

The Red Book recognised that, apart from small net profits in 1969 and 1970 as a result of capital reconstruction and the payment of grants for some loss-making but socially necessary services, BR had failed to pay its way, let alone earn sufficient money to finance fresh capital investment, since at least 1953.

It could, however, also point to some significant achievements: the 65% increase in passenger traffic since 1965 on the electrified routes from Euston to Manchester and Liverpool, evidence that there was a market for high-speed Inter-City services that justified the capital costs; a reduction of 33% in route mileage by the pruning of branch lines and by a half of the staff employed, which reflected a very substantial increase in productivity through better-planned use of manpower and modernisation of equipment.

But, and this is the nub of the case BR made, the main object of all legislation since 1947 had been to achieve viability and, with Dr Beeching's appointment in 1962, this had concentrated on the size of the network. While no one disputed the case for the pruning of many of the branch lines that had been axed, there was ample evidence that some of the closures, decided purely on theoretical profit-and-loss calculations of lines taken in isolation, had in practice lost traffic and revenue for the so-called "profitable" lines. Yet this was the course being again urged on the Board. An elaborate computer analysis of all possible permutations of network size and passenger/freight traffic was carried out and proved conclusively that all contractions of service or the size of the network greatly reduced the density of traffic on the surviving lines and thus increased their unit costs. For example, a halving of the network to around 5,000 route miles would certainly not produce viability and, would indeed, lead to greater loss. The Board thus confronted Peyton and the Government with the following bluntly-stated conclusion: "Within the present financial terms of reference, no railway network can be viable".

Their Chairman, Richard Marsh, put it thus:

In the last analysis we found that we could not even afford to shut the whole system up since the cost of redundancy and everything else associated with such an extreme step would cost far more than maintaining a loss-making railway system. Having decided there was no prospect whatever of an economically viable system, we asked, "What is the truly necessary railway?" We then told the Government they must accept the fact that there were no benefits from cutting the system and that it must be accepted that the social benefit to the community as a whole by keeping it intact was far greater than the book-keeping loss.

Whitehall – the Government that is – had to say either we were wrong in our assessment, over-rule our advice and order a cut-down – and accept the financial consequences; or alternatively accept the judgment of those who had been appointed by them to run the railways.

Marsh's words carried particular authority, for as Minister of Transport in the Labour Government he had been largely responsible for the 1968 Transport Act, with its reiteration of the goal of commercial viability. About that, after two years as BR Chairman he now candidly admits that he, like his Ministerial predecessors, had been wrong.

First a word about the man who led BR through this critical turning point. On deciding to abandon politics after Labour's defeat, Richard Marsh was appointed to BR as Chairman by his Conservative ministerial successor and political opponent John Peyton. For Marsh it was a further step in a remarkable career that had taken him in less than twenty years from being a young trade union organiser first to Westminster as a Member of Parliament, and then to become one of the youngest Cabinet ministers for 200 years. His appointment as Chairman inevitably aroused controversy and there were some in the industry who were doubtful about having a former politician rather than a professional railwayman at their head. But it also meant that for a very difficult time, when BR's future lay in the balance, they were led by a man with intimate knowledge of the Whitehall departments the Board were dealing with, and also of the world of politics.

He and Peyton, although poles apart politically, rapidly established a close working relationship. While Peyton made no secret of his dislike of nationalisation, he also took the view that his job was to make the system work efficiently and to trust the ability and judgment of those appointed to manage it with the minimum of political interference. He proved to have a clear analytical mind and won the confidence and respect of railway officers. Once convinced of the validity of their case – the turning-point came at a day-long seminar at BR headquarters, chaired by Peyton and involving management, Board members and senior civil servants – he put the case successfully to his Cabinet colleagues and then to Parliament.

In his statement to the Commons on 28 November 1973, Peyton confirmed that the existing 11,500-mile network would be retained. He added:

> I propose a switch of resources within the transport sector mainly from urban road to rail, to provide the necessary investment for the railways.
>
> This will increase over the next five years from some £140 million in 1973–74 to £225 million in 1977–78, which includes provision for the initial stages of a rail link to the Channel Tunnel. The Government will also continue to provide substantial revenue support to the railways

The total investment was estimated at £891m., and the operating subsidy had yet to be calculated, but the programme envisaged:

1. Loss-making, grant-aided passenger services being retained on social and environmental grounds.
2. Inter-City services improved, with the introduction of high-speed trains on the London–Bristol/South Wales route, and further development of the 155 m.p.h. advanced passenger train.
3. Improvement for "long-suffering commuters" with more electrification on

suburban services, new rolling-stock, better interchanges and modern passenger terminals.

4. Improved rail freight and parcel services with computer-controlled wagon movement and high-capacity wagons to give faster turnround times and greater reliability.

5. Increased investment in track and signalling on the key parts of the system to give higher safety and efficiency standards.

It was indicative of the new climate of public opinion that this statement, and particularly the cutdown on road-building, provoked little controversy: even the normally vociferous motoring organisations were comparatively quiet. Within three months, Peyton and the Conservatives were out of office and it fell to another minister, Fred Mulley, and a Labour Government to quantify the cost and conditions of the new policy – which they fully accepted. This emerged in the Railways Bill, published on 13 June 1974: up to £1,500m. would be available over the next five years as support costs for the passenger railway based on the existing network; a cut of £189m. in the Board's capital liabilities to the Secretary of State; the promise of grants to encourage industry to build private sidings and terminal facilities at factories adjacent to rail services in order to take freight off the roads. Not least significant about these two statements was that British Rail was at long last out of the political cockpit, with both parties agreed on its future. Satisfactory as it was, nonetheless Marsh felt able only to give it "a qualified welcome", and two points in particular concerned the Board: the size of its future capital investment programme and the future relationship between Whitehall and the Board. The Bill gave no undertaking to support the massive capital investment programme required to continue the modernisation of track signalling and the introduction of high-speed trains, and it also indicated that the Government intended to supervise closely the Board's long-term planning – just how detailed this would be was not clear. As Marsh pointed out, the capital investment the Board could afford from its own resources did little more than cover the replacement of worn-out equipment, and he believed that at least £1,000m. of fresh investment was required over the next five years. It was evident that the Treasury and the Transport Ministry were not going to part with money on the scale envisaged without a voice in how it was spent. The Board feared, with good reason from its past experiences, that this would lead to still further bureaucratic interference, delay, and unacceptable control over management's responsibilities. The existing controls, particularly the refusal of the Treasury to authorise capital spending for more than a year ahead, already seriously impeded long-term planning as well as increased costs for BR and their suppliers, who wanted to be able to plan their deployment of resources with some assurance about its future. It was a point that had been made many times over the years, which Peyton had certainly grasped. But his successor was either unable to grasp it or failed to persuade the Treasury that multi-million pound projects in a business enterprise could not be handled on the basis of Treasury regulations.

It was, for example, late summer 1974 before Whitehall decided on the spending it would approve in 1975; Marsh once estimated that the costs of some programmes could be reduced by as much as 25% had they been able to enter into long-term guaranteed contracts. And Peyton cites as an example of the impossibility of working within Whitehall's financial framework the case of a major new signalling installation which was delayed because the Treasury insisted on the cost of some minor work required to complete it being held over to the following financial year.

A Confident Base

By 1974, BR could look forward to a more stable and self-assured future. It stood in higher public esteem; the social and economic role that railways had to play had been recognised and accepted; there was a buoyancy and enthusiasm in its approach to the public through advertising and increasingly in staff morale, while management had been strengthened and the organisation slimmed down. As Richard Marsh puts it: "In the nineteenth century we were the king who first moved people faster than the horse could go; then there was the music-hall stage in the mid-twentieth century when we were dirty, inefficient and old-fashioned; now it is recognised that we are an essential part of the transport infrastructure". In two particular areas there had been notable successes. The first was the development of the Inter-City passenger services with ever-improving standards of accommodation, including air-conditioning, and higher speeds. By 1974 the completion of the West-Coast electrification from Preston to Glasgow – inaugurated by the Queen and the Duke of Edinburgh – linked London and Glasgow in five hours, at an average speed of 80 m.p.h. A year earlier the 1973 timetables incorporated many improved timings such as London to Newcastle, 268 miles in 210 minutes, and the fastest-ever schedule for the "Flying Scotsman", covering the 393 miles between King's Cross and Edinburgh in $5\frac{1}{2}$ hours at an average speed of over 71 m.p.h. In all, 200 Inter-City expresses were scheduled at an average speed of 70 m.p.h. or more every day. Secondly, where freight was concerned, although the general level continued to fall, there had been major advances in several fields for which railways were particularly suited, with trains of up to 1,000 tons carrying oil and petrol from refineries to inland distribution centres, and loads of cement, steel, iron ore, minerals, chemicals, and road-building materials. Ironically, the motor-car industry had also become a major rail user; a regular service of company trains between Ford's works in Dagenham and Liverpool, for example, was virtually part of the production-line belt, while rail was increasingly being used for the transport of finished cars from factories to the ports or regional distribution centres.

For a long time the biggest single handicap affecting reliability and an expansion of railways was the unhappy state of industrial relations and the number of strikes and interruptions of services. In part, the unrest reflected the relatively low pay of railway workers, but it was also complicated by the internecine warfare between the two main rail unions, ASLEF and the NUR; the former and smaller union had been steadily declining both in numbers and in prestige with the reduction in footplate staff and in the change in status that inevitably followed the transition from steam to diesel and electric traction. For over a century the engine-driver had been the elite, not only of railwaymen but of the working class – comparatively higher paid and secure in a job reached after years of arduous work as a cleaner and then as a fireman. To become a "top link" driver and take the "Flying Scotsman" out of King's Cross was to attain the height of professional achievement. It is not to disparage the skill and devotion of the driver of an electric or diesel locomotive travelling at speeds undreamt of in the days of steam, but the reality, which ASLEF were loth to recognise, is that the level of skill and responsibility is very different. Whereas the safety and speed of a steam train depended on the watchfulness of the driver and the partnership on the footplate between him and his fireman in creating and using the steam produced in the locomotive's boiler, the diesel or electric driver has little more to do than regulate the power provided by the generator or overhead wire, while automatic train control and modern signalling have increasingly replaced personal responsibility. The ASLEF leaders fought tenaciously, and at times irresponsibly, for their rights, and early in 1974 there was widespread disruption of services, particularly in the Southern Region, by strike action. For over a year they stopped trials of the experimental high-speed Advanced Passenger Train over a dispute about special payments for driving it. However, by autumn 1974 the Board and the unions had reached an agreement on pay and a restructuring of salary scales that seemed to herald a more settled future for the industry.

The Future

At this point, with the hope of a more stable political and industrial future, we can look at the prospects – and challenges – ahead as British Rail celebrates the 150th anniversary of the opening of the Stockton & Darlington Railway. What is so remarkable is how little, until the past generation or so, the basic technology pioneered by Stephenson has been changed. Over the years, the steam engine certainly grew bigger and more powerful, but the principles remained the same until eventually it gave way to diesel and electric power.

By the mid-sixties, steam had virtually disappeared from Britain but, more flexible and economic as diesel or electric traction might be, speed barriers had not risen significantly, an average from perhaps 50 to 70 m.p.h., with 100 m.p.h. still the ceiling apart from one or two experimental services in France and on the Tokaido line in Japan where, on a specially built track, regular services of about 130 m.p.h. were achieved. In face of ever-increasing competition, both in speed and service, from the airlines on the one hand and the rapidly expanding motorway network on the other, the railways had either to advance beyond Stephenson's nineteenth-century technology or admit defeat. There was no lack of mourners in waiting or bankruptcies among private railways in the United States.

Speed, as the Tokaido line had demonstrated, could be achieved on a purpose-built straight line, but to contemplate replacing thousands of miles of conventional track to achieve this in Britain was clearly unrealistic. On that line the cost, in terms of wear and tear in using conventional motive power and carriages, has proved massive; but it is closed nightly for inspection, while carriage wheels have to be re-profiled every ten days. The maintenance cost is clearly astronomical. The detrimental hammer-blow effect of heavy unsprung weights on the track increases dramatically as speeds rise – as does wheel wear. A possible alternative that seemed attractive was the hovertrain, utilising the techniques developed in Britain of propelling seacraft on a cushion of air on the water's surface. Experiments showed it was technically feasible, but very costly since it would have involved the construction of new routes duplicating the existing rail network. Research into the hovertrain project was abandoned by the Government in 1973.

A decade earlier, in 1962, British Rail had opened a research and development centre in Derby to explore the application of modern technology to railways. It was run on a shoestring and much suspected by traditional railway engineers but it was a welcome, if long overdue, recognition of the need for technical change and advance if railways were to survive the challenge. To meet this challenge, there came into railway research Dr Sydney Jones, a scientist with a career in aeronautics and guided missile research. He made the move because, as he put it, "there was an industry crying out for the application of modern science". It was a daunting prospect to contemplate transforming an industry so deeply rooted in traditional ways, nor was it easy to attract other scientists to an industry that seemed broken down, an archaic nineteenth-century survival compared with the excitement and drama of the air. "I wanted men from the aircraft industry able to apply their knowledge of dynamics to rail, because this was the central problem: how to move a train on the surface at very high speeds and keep it stable."

The development, from the humble beginning, of the Derby research centre is an exciting story. Dr Jones recruited his scientists and engineers from the aeroplane and other high-technology industries. Together the team set out to evaluate the potential inherent in the railway and to compare this with superficially more exciting alternative routes to high-speed ground transportation such as the air-cushioned hovertrains. The outcome was a decision to concentrate on the solution which offered the greatest return on investment – provided science could achieve it. That decision was to develop to the ultimate the railway system.

It is no exaggeration to say that the work of the Derby research team is comparable to that of the nineteenth-century pioneers who harnessed steam: they broke through the rail technology barrier and Derby is now acknowledged as the world's leading centre in high-speed rail research and development.

It took eighteen months of fundamental analysis, using the very latest computer techniques and laboratory methods, to arrive at an understanding of the fundamental principles involved when a flanged wheel railway wagon rolls on steel rails and to define them mathematically.

As previous experience with guided missiles had shown, the dynamics of the system are such that above certain speeds the forces which up to that point provided guidance and stability conspire to render the system unstable. The Derby team were able to report that considerable speed improvements were possible on existing railway lines by further development of vehicle suspension systems which would harness the very forces currently providing the limitation.

Given the ability to construct new tracks, the team were able to predict that wheels on rails could offer speeds around 250 m.p.h. whilst providing compatibility with existing tracks to gain access to city centres. This was competition indeed for the alternative high-speed ground transport systems such as hover-trains whose virtues were being extolled at the time but whose dependence on untried fundamentals left their practicability open to doubt.

It is interesting to note that in 1974 Derby's services were called upon by the Americans to provide dynamics consultancy for a project which required keeping a flange-wheeled railway vehicle firmly on the rails at speeds over 280 m.p.h. Alan Wickens, an original member of Dr Jones's team and now Director of the Derby Laboratories, commented: "The results obtained from the US tests are of great interest to us, confirming as they do many of the theoretical conclusions we had reached about the ability to operate conventionally guided railway vehicles at speeds around 250 m.p.h."

By 1969 the team had solved the theoretical problems of designing a suspension system to run at 155 m.p.h. on existing tracks, providing enough stopping power to halt the trains within the limitations of the existing signalling system, and had developed a coach tilting system which would maintain passenger comfort during high-speed curving.

The major problem was cash – even though by most technological project standards of the time the cost was relatively small. BR, in its straitened circumstances, had none to spare for the financing of what to the older generation of managers and engineers seemed fantasies. Eventually Dr Jones persuaded Sir Solly Zuckerman, then scientific adviser to the Cabinet, that the APT was feasible and he, in turn, persuaded the Government to finance its development on a 50–50 basis with the BR Board.

See Plate 58

Design and development of a train to prove the theoretical studies started in 1969 and was completed by 1972; by June the following year APT-E (Experimental) started running largely on a test track in Nottinghamshire and subsequently on some main lines, and it has fulfilled to a remarkably high degree the theoretical calculations worked out in the laboratory. At 135 m.p.h., even on the sharpest bends, its riding quality has proved as good as the best conventional coach running at much lower speeds on a straight line; it has proved able to remain stable as a result of the tilting of the body – up to nine degrees – on bends, without causing any discomfort or sense of lateral movement to passengers. The light alloy construction of the carriages produced a lightweight train; the hydro-kinetic brakes could rapidly bring it to a halt.

One important policy change was made as development continued. Although

APT-E was powered by gas turbines – partly for convenience in testing without a dependence on overhead electric supply systems, and partly to provide experience of operating with and developing this form of traction – a number of factors favoured electric traction for the APT's first commercial services. With the settlement of the ASLEF dispute in 1974, full-scale testing was able to go ahead. By the end of the year the test speed was raised to 155 m.p.h., the maximum envisaged – initially at any rate – for the APT in service, although its designers are confident that speeds up to 200 m.p.h. could be attained. The experimental carriages contain a massive array of computers and electronic equipment that will make it the most thoroughly tested train ever designed.

The electric prototype APTs will go into service in 1977–8, first on the West Coast main line, giving a journey time between London and Glasgow of four hours, compared with five hours now, at an average speed of just under 100 m.p.h. In appearance, the APT will be as revolutionary as it is technically, with a wedge-shaped front end, a curving roof and body made from lightweight aluminium, more akin in shape to an aircraft than a conventional railway carriage, with the gaps between its twelve carriages covered in, to form a continuous surface.

To retain and further develop Inter-City traffic before the introduction of the APT, BR developed the High Speed Train, in part a technological spin-off from research on the APT, but in practice a "stretched" version of the conventional diesel-powered train. It will come into regular 125 m.p.h. service in 1977. The HST, driven by two 2,250 horse-power engines, is less revolutionary than the APT and, of course, has none of the latter's advanced technology. It is somewhat similar in appearance, though rather more square-shaped at the front; like the APT its power unit is incorporated in the train rather than in a separate locomotive. The HST will have 75-ft carriages – 9 ft longer than existing ones – with full air-conditioning and sound proofing.

Strategy for the 1980s

While the APT originated in a scientist's dream, the HST was the result of a long-term planning decision taken in 1970 that, in order to meet air and road competition, speeds had to be substantially increased. Experience with electrification on the London–Manchester–Liverpool lines had shown that on journeys of up to $2\frac{1}{2}$ hours or so – say 200–250 miles – rail could compete with, and even defeat, air competition in what the passenger needs: namely, a quick and comfortable, regular and reliable service for city-to-city journeys. The airways might claim a 45-minute journey between London and Manchester, but the reality is that the overall journey to the traveller's final destination takes very much longer, to say nothing of the inconvenience of movement from terminals to airports, with the same performance repeated at the other end. Although rail, like air, is at the mercy of the weather, it is a great deal less so; it affords a properly-cooked meal rather than a rushed plastic concoction, and leg-room and time to work or read without interruption. Domestic flights between Manchester and London fell by 30% in the year after electrification and have continued to stagnate or decline ever since, while rail journeys have steadily risen until, in 1974, BR commanded 85% of the rail–air traffic. A very high proportion of it is first-class business travel, but a combination of fast regular services, combined with cheap-rate fares for day or weekend travel, created a new market amongst those who would not otherwise have travelled at all. The London–Manchester line carried 865,700 passengers in 1973 compared with 518,300 in the year prior to electrification. The same pattern on other routes, with either electric or diesel Inter-City services, has developed, while the growth of the motorway network did not appear to have a significant effect on total rail carryings.

Rail was clearly dominant both against air and, to a lesser extent, road journeys of up to about 250 miles (or $2\frac{1}{2}$–3 hours' travel time), as well as in specialised services over long distances, where the sleeping car could meet the businessman's needs for at least one leg of his journey. A programme to modernise the stock of sleeping cars and improve the facilities available was introduced. The car-carrying services – Motorail – which BR had pioneered in 1956 and which have since been developed by every European railway – catered for the long-distance holidaymaker who wanted his car at his resort but not the trouble and often expense involved when distance required a break in a journey at a hotel. A special Motorail Terminal was opened at Kensington (Olympia) station and by 1974 there were 43 services linking most of the holiday centres or Channel ports with either London or major provincial centres: they carried over 200,000 passengers and 90,000 cars.

See Plate 63

It was, however, evident that rail's superiority declined rapidly on journeys lasting over the $2\frac{1}{2}$–3 hours. Improvement in track, notably on the East Coast line, and the elimination of speed restrictions by, for example, re-aligning tracks and rebuilding stations at notorious bottlenecks such as Peterborough and to a lesser extent at Durham, secured some paring of journey times. But the reality had to be faced that by 1980 journey times would be little different from those of a decade earlier, with an ageing fleet of diesel locomotives limited to 100 m.p.h. By no stretch of the imagination could, say, Newcastle be brought into the $2\frac{1}{2}$–3 hour orbit, while the possible development of Vertical or Short Take-off planes could counteract the disadvantages of airports and terminals at long distances from city centres. If, as a consequence, the rail market stagnated, there would be less capital available for new investment and the vicious circle of the fifties and sixties would emerge again with probably even more disastrous consequences. The target the engineers and designers were set was Newcastle in three hours, Edinburgh in four hours – not just by a few selected elite expresses at premium fares such as the Continental TEEs, but as the standard operating performance and at half-hourly intervals on the main trunk routes. From this, the HST emerged. This is diesel-powered, using conventional, although unproved and longer, coaches. To limit weight, there are seven coaches only per train, a reduction achieved in part by eliminating separate restaurant-car and kitchen carriages and providing passengers with meals at their seats from a single kitchen equipped with micro-air ovens. The shorter journey times will enable each train set to be used more intensively; up to three or four round trips daily, of 500 miles each, become possible. The following table shows the reduction in journey times planned with HST and APT compared with 1974 schedules.

	Now 90/100 m.p.h. mins	HST 125 m.p.h. mins	APT 155 m.p.h mins
London to:			
Newcastle	212	180	140
Leeds	150	127	105
Glasgow	300	–	240
Manchester	146	–	120
Cardiff	135	104	86
Bristol	110	83	67

Having developed both HST and APT, the next strategic question to be settled was when to use them and which routes to give priority to, and a rolling pro-gramme through to the mid-1980s has been evolved. The London–Glasgow line, with its many bends, is ideally suited for the APT with its ability to round curves at high speed, but produces less benefit for the HST since there are few stretches where 125 m.p.h. could be sustained for long enough to give worthwhile saving in time. On the other hand, the straight, well-graded and comparatively short route from Paddington to Bristol and South Wales enables the HST to be exploited to the full, so much so that only at over 155 m.p.h. would APT provide any significant saving in time on these routes. The first HST services will, therefore, begin operating here in 1976 and the construction of the first 27 sets, at a cost of £850,000 each, is now under way. Forty-four sets are planned for the East Coast from King's Cross to Newcastle and Edinburgh in 1978, to be followed by principal cross-country routes (Newcastle–Bristol–Plymouth and Edinburgh–Glasgow). A building programme of 30 sets a year is planned.

The APT production trains will therefore be introduced first on the West Coast line in the early 1980s and will then replace HSTs on the East Coast, Bristol/South Wales and finally the West of England line to Plymouth by about 1985 – thus completing within about a decade a total transformation of main-line rail passenger transport in Britain.

The key to these developments rests in the extent to which the Government is prepared to authorise electrification of the main trunk routes to enable the conventional and ageing diesel locomotives to be phased out and eventually the APT to supersede the HST. Britain has a lower proportion of electrified track than most European nations – 19% compared with 24% in France, 28% in West Germany and 48% in Italy – with two-thirds of it in the South-East and Euston–Glasgow as the only major trunk route. Work should be completed on 73 miles of the Great Northern suburban services from King's Cross by 1977 and design work is in hand for the lines from St Pancras to Bedford, Bishops Stortford to Cambridge, and Colchester to Harwich, Ipswich, and Felixstowe. The latter two would eliminate the uneconomic mixture of diesel and electric traction in East Anglia and with an electrified link across London would give improved freight services from the industrial north to Harwich and Felixstowe, the two major docks for trade with Europe.

The piecemeal approach that has characterised post-war electrification planning increases costs when skilled teams of designers and engineers are disbanded only to be subsequently reformed, and the expertise that BR and their contractors have developed is inevitably diluted.

Electrification of the East-Coast route from King's Cross to Edinburgh and the main route from Paddington to South Wales and the West Country could be achieved at a fraction of the cost of building new motorways with, as the Euston electrification has shown, immense benefits to travellers and BR.

Another major electrification project is, of course, connected with the Channel Tunnel, but plans for building a high-speed line from the tunnel portals at Cheriton to a new Continental terminus at White City in west London were abandoned by the Government in November 1974 when the Environment Minister, Anthony Crosland, told the Commons that the estimated cost had risen from £120m. in 1973 to £373m. in 1974, largely as a result of inflation, and that the Government could not authorise expenditure of this size. He recognised the importance of a rail link from the Tunnel to London, giving freight and passenger trains access to the main BR routes to the north; but a cheaper way of doing it had to be found before decision to go ahead with the Tunnel itself could be taken. The scheme Crosland rejected had envisaged a completely new line from the coast through Kent, going underground beneath the Thames, and then to the White City terminal for London-bound travellers, where the existing cross-London lines connect with the main trunk routes to the West, North-West and North-East.

Presumably what the Government had in mind was to utilise the existing Dover–Ashford–Victoria line for the cross-Channel trains, although it is very doubtful if this route – intensively worked already, particularly in the outer suburban area – could cope with the extra traffic or Victoria Station become the London terminal without rebuilding and enlargement; nor is it easy to see how the existing surface line from Clapham Junction to White City could carry the volume of traffic if the under-London tunnel is rejected. Crosland's statement was seen by many MPs as casting doubts on the willingness of the Government to go ahead with the Channel Tunnel itself. An Anglo-French agreement in principle was signed in 1973 and due to be ratified in 1975, and the French Government remain anxious to go ahead with it. But at best the dream, first mooted in 1802 and revived innumerable times since then, has been delayed, and all the work by Channel Tunnel companies (in which BR and the French Railways are in partnership with private interests), as well as BR's own planning of schedules for services from London and the major provincial centres to Europe, is in suspense.

Looking Ahead

There is little doubt that the APT can be stretched to 250 m.p.h., to bring
Newcastle a mere 100 minutes from London, and Edinburgh two and a half
hours, although it would require further and costly improvements in track and
signalling which might not be justified in a country where distances are comparatively short.

In determining priorities we have to consider the shape of Britain in the year
2000 – how its population will be spread and what its transport needs will be.
But with a long life-span and massive capital investment such as railways required,
and when equipment may last twenty-five years and tracks a century or more, the
necessity to look ahead is obvious, albeit into the crystal ball at times. The
fallibility of forecasting is all too vividly illustrated by the 1973 oil crisis which
reversed all post-war planning, and the same has been true, although perhaps less
dramatically, of railways. Nonetheless there are broad trends discernible which
can guide long-term planning.

The most important single one is that on current estimates of population
there will be 9 million people more in these islands by the year 2000, the
equivalent, unless they are to be packed into the already overstretched Midlands
and South-East conurbations, of 60 new towns each of 150,000 people. At the
same time, social changes will have far-reaching impacts on travel patterns.
There will be more leisure time, an increase in two-house ownership and more
young people in further education away from home. Personal transport will
undoubtedly continue to expand, whether it is the car – that symbol of individual
independence – or the moped, that gives the young freedom to move cheaply
and quickly. As prosperity grows, the demand for transport increases, with more
people on the move and more freight to be transported from factory to consumer
or to ports for export abroad.

In 1973 the Road Research Laboratory estimated that, on the current trends,
the number of cars will have risen to 18 million by 1980 and 26 million by the
end of the century, and lorries to about 2·3 million. And with it there will be an
inevitable and devastating increase in road accidents and a massive increase in
the cost of the roads and motorways needed to cope with this volume of traffic.
Motorway building costs (at 1974 prices) were between £1·5m. a mile in rural
areas and £15m. a mile in urban areas, the latter often involving destruction of
property and environmental pollution.

It was a combination of cost and public opinion that in 1973 forced the
Greater London Council to abandon plans for a motorway box on the capital's
outskirts, and these pressures are likely to grow in the years ahead. Yet simply to
halt the progress of the motorway without providing an alternative can only
lead to strangulation, and the danger that, as Richard Marsh has warned us,
industry will find it cannot move freight on the scale required in a decade from
now because it will have neither the road nor the rail capacity. That is equally
true of the commuter problem in London and other major urban centres, and is

paralleled in many other western countries. It is at its most acute in Britain because of the massive concentration of population in the South-East; but Los Angeles, a lasting monument to the dream of a motorised society and six-lane urban motorways, has rush hours when nothing moves. It is the United States that is now pressing hardest for the development of rapid-transit rail transport, as in the commuter area around San Francisco or, for longer journeys, seizing on the potential of the APT – demonstrated by the agreement with British Rail to share in the "know-how" of its development.

Long-range forecasts of the growth in motor and air transport have inevitably been affected by the oil crisis; the threatened shortage may not materialise but the very much higher prices seem certain to stay and must significantly further improve rail's potential competitiveness.

Let us first take the implication of the APT combined with future population growth. Should the primary aim be to press on from 150 to 250 m.p.h., as is undoubtedly technically feasible? Or should social policy, with in particular housing and new town development, be related to what APT at 150 m.p.h. can contribute? The attractions of going for even higher speeds are considerable, but it is arguable that the time-saving, balanced against cost, cannot be justified except possibly on the West Coast line. The 150 m.p.h. APT, on the other hand, opens up new dimensions in town planning and location. Experience has shown that an hour's commuting time – or even more – is perfectly acceptable and that the distance involved is secondary; with electrification, towns such as Southampton, 70–80 miles out of London but linked with fast regular services, have come into the commuting range; with APT, satellite towns, partly self-contained but primarily serving the main industrial centres and up to 150 miles away, become feasible: for example, in the vast open areas of the Scottish Highlands rather than in the already overcrowded industrial belt between Glasgow and Edinburgh. The primary target that some BR planners believe should be aimed at in the next twenty years is to link all major cities and these new towns with a half-hourly 150 m.p.h. service. Whether Government and social planners are yet fully aware of the revolution that APT opens up is another question.

The Freight Scene

The transport pattern is constantly changing. The discovery of North Sea oil has transformed the economics of north-east Scotland and the lines north of Aberdeen to Inverness, Thurso and Wick, only a few years ago regarded as candidates for closure, are rapidly becoming vital links with the south for both freight and passenger traffic. Ever-increasing air fares, as a result of the oil crisis, are changing the competitive balance even more markedly than with road transport. But the central problem, both for BR's economics and for the contribution rail can – and should – make to the nation's economy lies in freight traffic. In 1974, rail in the UK carried a smaller proportion of total freight movement than in any other West European nation, and its share was steadily declining for a variety of reasons, some of which were political, others economic, and also in part because of the industry's failure to provide competitive services. The comparatively short distances favoured the road while many years of Government control over rail freight charges prevented the railways from competing with road haulage until the 1960s when BR was given greater commercial freedom. The decline of coal, steel and heavy engineering undermined the traditional base of rail freight traffic, and showed how ill-equipped was rail to satisfy the transport requirements of light industry. BR had achieved a reputation for unreliability and high costs, particularly for general merchandise. It is true that in some specific areas, such as the Freightliners, the bulk transport of oil, cement, car distribution or the development of company trains linking, say, factories, BR had effectively demonstrated rail's ability to provide a better and cheaper service than road – significant as a pointer to what can be achieved but nonetheless comparatively small.

See Plates 65, 66 and 67

Another factor has been political: the pressure from the road-haulage interests on a Conservative Government ideologically inclined to see the issue in terms of a battle between private enterprise and a nationalised monopoly. The road-haulage industry can, and does, very vehemently point to the fact that of the 2,000 million tons of UK freight transported annually, rail carried a mere 10%, which could easily be transferred to road. But the reality is very different. The greater part of the country's freight traffic, some 1,200 million tons, travels far less than 25 miles, for which there is no sensible alternative to road transport. But at the other extreme, the medium- to long-distance lorry, and the real cause of public concern, some 200 million tons are carried by road over 50 miles. It is in this area and not in local delivery that the real clash of interest arises, which can only be resolved by Government decisions about the future balance of transport.

There are two courses open to BR: to concentrate on the bulk movement of raw materials in 1,000-ton train loads and, apart from specialised services such as the Red Star express parcels delivery, surrender general freight traffic to the road hauliers; alternatively to develop services capable of satisfying a much wider range of needs, thus combining the inherent advantages of rail with the flexibility of road haulage. The latter can be achieved by compulsion, State-imposed restrictions on road hauliers through licensing or limitations on length of journeys, that would force industrialists to use rail for all except the short-haul traffic. But experience has demonstrated that controls of this sort simply do not work or, if they are to be made effective, require a massive army of bureaucrats to enforce them. The simple truth is that unless rail can satisfy the needs of industry – its customers – it cannot survive. There are some marginal areas where Government controls could justifiably be introduced to limit long-distance road haulage, while the pressure of costs will certainly affect the competitive balance between road and rail in the latter's favour, and over the next two decades some form of road pricing may be introduced to discourage both the motorised commuter in urban areas and the long distance road haulier.

British Rail, to judge by the Railway Policy Review assessment of their future as freight hauliers, appear at first sight to take a pessimistic view of their prospects.

They assume that by the year 2000 they will carry no more than the 200 million tons they carried in 1974, in spite of the growth in industrial production which, at even the most conservative estimates, can be anticipated. The figures, however, masked the fact that the prospects were viewed against a very fast declining coal industry, against which there was a substantial gain in tonnage of other freight to compensate. Also the estimates were based on the railways' role as seen under the 1968 Transport Act.

With the financial inducements to be offered to industry for the development of private sidings under the new Railways Act 1974, and the Government's new energy policy which at least arrests the previously forecast rapid decline in coal production, the prospects are now very much brighter for higher rail freight tonnages, especially as the pattern of traffic will change, with the balance moving towards bulk haulage.

There now appear to be positive indications of an entirely different situation in which, with a probable doubling of ton miles by the year 2000, a doubling of rail freight carryings by that time could well be contemplated, especially if terms of reference are adjusted to reflect external economic and social factors.

The central weakness in BR's freight service has been its inflexibility and lack of effective managerial control; a story of wagons disappearing apparently into the blue, customers ignorant of the whereabouts of their goods, all combined with an unacceptably high level of costs. Even the Freightliners, although they carried about 700,000 containers in 1974 and represent a valuable contribution to reducing road traffic, make only a modest profit. A continuing expansion can be anticipated over the years ahead particularly as containerisation becomes the norm for sea freight. The Far East shipping lines will be almost wholly container-ised and the distribution of 230,000 containers a year from Southampton will be almost entirely by rail. Nonetheless, there is a need to develop a network of mini or joint terminals to supplement the existing twenty-five major ones as well as smaller containers and simpler, more economic transfers at the depots. The growth in private sidings could help overcome one of the major drawbacks to the Freightliner: the fact that the final leg of its journey is very often through urban areas and thus as objectionable in principle as the long-distance juggernaut. Another development on which research is being done is the self-propelled remote-controlled wagon utilising the guided track and able to be dispatched almost at will by its owner. There are many problems to be solved by assuming what is already feasible, namely completely automatic trains requiring no driver and regulated throughout their journey by computer, there is no reason why this could not be applied to individual wagons, provided such a service would be commercially viable.

In the meantime, as a step towards improving the flexibility of BR's freight services, the computer is being brought in to give management instantaneous control and knowledge of the nationwide situation by developing, at a cost of about £10m., TOPS – the Total Operating Processing System originally designed by an American railway, the Southern Pacific Transportation Company, who are advising BR on adapting it to British conditions. It operates on IBM System 370 Model 168 computers and has started in the West of England. When fully operational by the autumn of 1975 throughout BR it will be one of the largest real-time computer systems in the world. TOPS will consist of a comprehensive data base holding information on the location, contents and conditions of all rail freight vehicles and locomotives throughout the country. All depots, shunting yards and offices will be linked to it. The information will be immediately available either for customers or for operating staff, thus enabling them to plan train and traffic movement. BR believe that this will greatly improve their competitiveness in the freight market by giving a much higher standard of service and more efficient operation. In addition, it is planned to use some of the spare capacity of TOPS to control seat reservations on the HST and APT, enabling passengers to book a seat from a wide range of stations and, from BR's point of view, ensuring maximum use of accommodation.

Research and its Application

Costs, and this is at the heart of the rail's economic battle, depend on two things: manpower – the number of men required to drive trains or control their safe passage; and the track on which they run, which requires constant inspection and maintenance. The last decade has seen a major increase in productivity; higher speeds have meant better utilisation of locomotives and rolling-stock, with four long-distance journeys a day instead of two; automated signals and points have eliminated the need for a manned signal-box every two or three miles; ultrasonic

See Plates 70, 71 and 72 track-checking machines able to detect the minutest flaws have supplemented the linesman pacing his stretch of track each day. Twenty-five signal-boxes instead of 39 now control traffic between Waterloo and Southampton/Bournemouth and by 1978 the 396 miles from London to Edinburgh will be regulated by 30 power boxes instead of the 200 used twenty years ago. But there is scope for still greater automation and the use of less manpower. As already mentioned, the computer is

See Plate 73 coming in to control freight traffic; London Transport's Victoria Line, which was opened in 1968–9, is largely automated. But, in practice, a train operator is still employed on each Victoria Line train even though his duties consist of door operation and equipment monitoring rather than driving, and to drive the train in emergency. Here lies a real psychological problem: at present the traveller is so far not prepared to hand himself over to the automated train and the computer, and a driver provides a reassurance that there is a human being in charge should anything go wrong. The time may come when this will not be necessary. But far-reaching changes in train control are inevitable, and will be made inescapable when speeds approach the 200 m.p.h. mark.

REMOTE CONTROL

Present-day driving and control techniques rely on a combination of the signalling system and the driver's knowledge of the route to provide him with information about the line ahead. As traffic densities and speeds increase, the rate at which information must be supplied to him, and his ability to react and control his train, increases, and with it the risk of human error grows. Many of the landmarks, such as small stations or variations in track, that the driver used to rely on to navigate his course and keep a check on timings have disappeared or will become irrelevant at very high speeds. There are two alternative courses open if more effective train control is to be achieved: either to extend existing techniques – the modular approach – or to devise a control system which is complete in itself and replaces any existing one. This latter is the most effective for a new or totally rebuilt railway but is difficult to justify in an established system.

Research is going on under two principal heads: the driving function which is concerned with the movement of individual trains, and the traffic control function which covers their planning and operation. For the former the aim is to reduce the possibility of human error, to reduce the amount of route knowledge required by the driver, to minimise the effect of fog and bad weather and to reduce energy consumption by ensuring that trains are run at the most economic speeds. The traffic control function aims at supplementing the existing signalling system with computer information provided instantaneously to signalmen and traffic regulators about the state of traffic and position of all trains on a route.

There are a number of methods of remote control. At its simplest it is the Automatic Warning System (AWS) devised by the Great Western Railway and now installed on principal BR routes which gives the driver an audible and visual warning as he approaches a signal and automatically applies the brakes if he ignores a danger warning. This, combined with electronically controlled signalling from centralised signal-boxes, provides a high degree of safety and efficient control of the trains at conventional speeds. But for the future the primary aim is to ensure that the driver has a constant display of information as to the signals ahead and knowledge of his precise position at any moment, then to provide him with a computer-controlled programme that will regulate the speed, running times and station stops all in accordance with the timetable, as well as take into account any interruptions or delays that may occur to his or the preceding train.

The first question is how to ensure a constant and absolutely reliable link between the control centre and the train comparable to that achieved between ground controls and an aircraft. The danger of interference or interruption, for example, in tunnels produces problems for radio techniques. An alternative that has been investigated is using the running rails to transmit instructions to the driver but, while practical over comparatively short distances such as on the Victoria Line, the rail's poor transmission qualities eliminate this for long-distance main line routes. Also, there must be no interference with the existing signalling system. The most promising solution so far being developed lies in "track conductors", a two-wire transmission line laid between the running rails, through which messages are passed to receiving equipment on the train which in turn decodes and translates it into the information the driver requires. An experimental version of this system covering the advanced warning of signals is now in operation on two stretches of line in the Southern Region and has proved satisfactory. The next stage is to extend this to control of speeds and information about location, speed restrictions, etc. – the Speed Supervision System – which is now being tested under operating conditions at Wilmslow, near Manchester. These are thought adequate for the HST running at up to 125 m.p.h., but an additional problem arises with the APT travelling at 150 m.p.h. or more but operating in comparatively small numbers over a large mileage. The essential feature of this control mechanism is that the speed supervision information is stored both on the train and in the programme store on magnetic tapes. The information is furnished by transponders placed at regular intervals along the line as the APT progresses along its route, checked with the programme store and any necessary changes in speed communicated back to the driver. Parallel to this is the development of Automatic Train Reporting, which provides the controller with a constant flow of information checked by computer against the timetable and able to advise on the course to be taken to deal with any deviations. This is of particular importance where there are a large number of routes and traffic is heavy. Thus the capacity of the traffic controller to assess a given situation in time is inevitably limited, but a single delay can have quick repercussions over a wide area such as on the Southern Region's highly-concentrated and finely-timed services to and from London.

Trials of the first computerised traffic control system are planned for Glasgow Central Station, which has 13 platforms approached by six lines and complicated junctions. The computer will watch the sequence of trains and their platforming in order to keep the movements to the timetable and work out the best way of restoring services after any interruption. Preliminary studies suggest that these techniques could reduce delays in busy commuter areas by 50%.

All these developments mark a major break-through in the adaptation of electronic knowledge and computers to ensure safety at even higher speeds and increase operating efficiency; but communication to the train still depends on point-to-point trackside signalling. The signals may have become more efficient and the aids to the driver more comprehensive, but they are no different in principle from the basic concepts of the early days of railways. If the full benefits of automation are to be achieved, control of the speed of the train must be centralised: in other words, transferred from the driver to the central control point with instructions going direct to the power unit and thus obviating not only the need to employ a driver but even the need for a conventional signalling system.

A Total Automatic Control of Trains System (TACT) is being developed by British Rail and although, as already mentioned, it is unlikely to be practicable for application in Britain, it has an obvious potential either for new railways or for the modernisation of lines which have not yet been equipped with modern signalling and telecommunications, such as exist in developing countries. There is also scope for its application to automatic freight vehicles and commuter trains.

TRACK

The heart of any railway is the track, itself something which is expensive to maintain and, as trains get faster and heavier, subject to ever-increasing wear and tear. The basic track – steel lines pinned to sleepers laid on ballast – has remained unchanged through the century, although in the past decade concrete has replaced wood for the sleepers, whilst long-welded rails have replaced the jointed track and made for a smoother and quieter ride as well as reducing maintenance costs. But the future development may well lie in substituting for the ballast and sleepers a continuous concrete bed to which the lines are pinned and the first two trial tracks of this sort, at Radcliffe-on-Trent and Duffield, have demonstrated its feasibility, particularly for a new railway. The techniques of laying the concrete base to a high level of accuracy have been developed from machines originally used in motorway construction, and five years' experience has demonstrated that the stability and reliability at least equals the conventional tracks, while maintenance costs are far lower. But the drawback so far as the replacement of existing tracks is concerned is the length of time concrete takes to set before the rails can be fixed and traffic allowed to run. Investigations are continuing into the use of other materials which solidify more rapidly, such as asphalt, to replace concrete as the track foundation.

BATTERY TRACTION

Another major field of research is into lightweight batteries, being carried out at Derby in cooperation with the Atomic Energy Authority research centre at Harwell; a separate research programme has been launched by the Electricity Council and Chloride Ltd, who are the world's largest manufacturers of industrial batteries. The sodium sulphate battery was pioneered by the Ford Motor Company in America but has not yet been fully developed for commercial use. Being only a tenth of the weight of the traditional lead-acid battery, it has obvious potential for road vehicles. There is also considerable scope for its use on railways, replacing diesel-powered trains on branch lines and providing a complement for main-line electric locomotives. The West German railways have a number of conventional battery-operated trains, but their size and weight limit their effective use to very short distances, say some 10 miles.

The sodium sulphate battery, on the other hand, is capable of powering trains for up to 50 miles. It depends on the inter-action of molten sulphur and molten sodium at a temperature of 350°C, which poses technical problems, particularly in the field of advanced ceramics. These are regarded as well on the way to being overcome and within three years BR hope to have developed batteries capable of giving the power required at an economic cost. Both sodium and sulphur are easy to obtain, whilst lead is scarce, expensive, and heavy. Moreover, the batteries are fully sealed, require no maintenance, and are pollution-free.

Besides supplying power for branch-line trains as an alternative to diesels, they can be used in conjunction with either diesel-electric or fully electric locomotives. They would enable a smaller generator to be used on the former and, as an auxiliary power unit, they would increase the versatility of the latter. This would, for example, eliminate the need for costly overhead wiring of depots, marshalling yards and sidings in future electrification schemes, by giving the locomotive an independent source of power.

MANUFACTURE

British Rail Engineering Ltd is a subsidiary company of the Board, which controls what are still rather quaintly known as "railway workshops", although factories would be a more accurate title. BREL are, in fact, one of the largest engineering enterprises in the country, employing 39,000 people, and with a turnover of about £125m. a year and a growing export business. After years of retreat and decline, when the pre-nationalisation workshops were cut from 30 to 13 over 15 years and it was intended to reduce them still further, the tide turned in 1970 with the Government's commitment to large-scale modernisation of the railways. And the 1968 Transport Act gave BREL freedom to manufacture both for export and for home market customers as well as for British Rail.

About £17m. has been spent on modernising the factories, and BREL are now the only manufacturer of railway vehicles in Britain. Technical equipment, however, such as electric and diesel motors, is supplied by outside contractors like English Electric and General Electric, whilst the export business is done in partnership with Metro-Cammell of Birmingham. The choice for BREL when given freedom to go into the export business lay between setting up a separate overseas sales organisation or finding a partner, and Metro-Cammell, who have small manufacturing resources but great expertise in sales and overseas representation, proved to be the answer. By 1974 the partnership had £10m. worth of export orders on their books. Recent ones have included sales of 800 wagons to Yugoslavia, 65 EMU suburban coaches to Taiwan, and 140 wagons to Jordan. The capital investment now approved for BR over the next five years will inevitably lead to a further expansion in BREL workshops, while their growing success in exports should go some way to restore Britain's role in supplying overseas railway companies which has steadily declined in the post-war years.

No attempt to look into the future of British Rail would be complete without mention of London Transport and, indeed, the problem of transport in the major conurbations both here and overseas. The critical problem is how to move hundreds of thousands of commuters to and from work each day, and within their cities. London Transport and BR's commuter services carry about 1,200 million people a year and the great majority in a couple of hours in the mornings and evenings, with staff and capital investment idle for the greater part of the day. The same is true of every other major city, and all such undertakings share the difficulty of persuading people to stagger their working hours and of attracting staff willing to work on shift. A further problem is the movement of population from the urban centres to the outlying areas, which means that it is increasingly difficult to recruit staff.

London Transport's network of tracks and stations running deep under London and emerging into the suburbs began in 1863 as an extension of the main-line railways. In 1933 the separate rail companies and the bus, tram and trolleybus operators were merged into the London Passenger Transport Board, and the most comprehensive system of urban transport in the world. But it was only in the post-war years that there was a fresh look at the social and economic problems involved in urban transport. Out of this came the first new London underground line to be built across Central London for 62 years: the Victoria Line, running diagonally from Walthamstow in the north-east, linking three main-line termini (King's Cross, Euston and Victoria), going into the heart of London at Oxford Circus and then under the Thames to the densely populated south-east at Brixton.

By 1973 it was carrying 90 million passengers a year and more than satisfied the financial criteria required for public investment in urban transport facilities. And it did relieve pressure on other sections of the underground and on road traffic into London. The benefits are hard to quantify, but in the judgment of both London Transport and the Government departments involved, it has more than justified itself. In 1971 work started on the second new underground here – the Fleet Line, initially from Baker Street to the Strand with plans for further stages under the City of London to Fenchurch Street and out to the east, and on an extension of the Piccadilly Line from Hounslow to Heathrow Airport, which should be completed by 1977 and will provide a link for travellers from Central London to the airport in a journey time of about 35–40 minutes.

Although there have been joint studies and works programmes in the past, London's transport policy has sometimes tended to be dealt with piecemeal, with BR and LT pursuing their separate capital investment and pricing policies. The creation of Passenger Transport Executives, with control of both bus and rail services, has laid the way for coordinated planning and development of transport in the provinces and work began in 1974 on an underground railway in Newcastle linked to the existing suburban BR routes along the Tyne river. But in recent years it was not until the publication of the London Rail Study in December 1974 that the problems of London as a whole were looked at again. The survey, a joint project by the Greater London Council and the Department of the Environment, embraced what it called the "London Commuter Network", stretching from Bournemouth in the south-west to Bletchley in the north and Clacton in the east, an area covering some 10 million people and a thousand stations. It recommended the construction of the second stage of the Fleet line, a new River Line to the dockland area north of the Thames, which is now being redeveloped for housing as the inner London docks decline in importance, and also south of the Thames to Greenwich, Woolwich and Thamesmead. As a long-term project, there is also the proposal for a BR cross-rail line, linking Paddington and Liverpool Street north of the Thames, Victoria and Blackfriars and London Bridge to the south.

In technical terms, the most critical problem facing London Transport railways is a combination of manpower shortage and public opinion. Trains can be run automatically, timetabled and controlled by computers, as the Victoria Line has demonstrated, but the Government and the travelling public want the reassurance of a human link, and the full benefits of modern technology cannot yet be realised. Still, within a year or two it is planned to introduce one-man working on the Circle and Hammersmith and City Lines as a step towards complete automation; in economic terms this will represent a major saving in manpower, while every step towards completely automatic running makes the operation more flexible and less dependent on shifts and staff availability.

Conclusion

As British Rail celebrate their anniversary they can look to the future with greater optimism than for many years past. The long years of decline have been halted and both in Britain and abroad there is a new awareness of the role that railways can and must provide in modern industrialised societies. Far from being a nineteenth-century anachronism in the age of cars and planes they have the potential to solve many of the transport problems that the internal combustion engine has created, and to do so often more cheaply and efficiently. As this survey has shown, British Rail are at the threshold of dramatic advances in speed and the bulk movement of freight, with advanced technology being exploited in every area of railway operations. The Stockton & Darlington Railway helped to produce a revolution that spread through the world. The work that British Rail's scientists, engineers and planners have done in the past decade has opened up a new Railway Era, one that will transform the system by the year 2000 and put Britain once again in the lead in railway engineering and development.

A Note On Books
Index

A NOTE ON BOOKS

The history of railways needs to be seen first as a part of the general history of transport. For that there are two authorities of outstanding value: W. T. Jackman, *The Development of Transportation in Modern England* (2 vols., 1916), which treats the subject in detail down to 1850, and H. J. Dyos and D. H. Aldcroft, *British Transport* (Pelican ed., 1974).

The most useful general history of British railways is C. H. Ellis, *British Railway History* (2 vols., 1954–59). See also J. Simmons, *The Railways of Britain* (2nd ed., 1968), R. M. Robbins, *The Railway Age* (Penguin ed., 1965), and H. Perkin, *The Age of the Railway* (1970). A detailed history down to 1852 is afforded by H. G. Lewin in *Early British Railways* (1925) and *The Railway Mania and its Aftermath* (1936). Among Victorian works two are of special value: J. Francis, *History of the English Railway* (2 vols., 1851), and (Sir) W. M. Acworth, *The Railways of England* (5th ed., 1900), with the same author's *Railways of Scotland* (1890). The large literature of the subject is catalogued in G. Ottley, *Bibliography of British Railway History* (1965). A recent work of importance on the economic history is R. G. R. Hawke, *Railways and Economic Growth in England and Wales, 1840–70* (1970). There is no general history of railway labour, but that of the National Union of Railwaymen is described in P. S. Bagwell, *The Railwaymen* (1963).

The locomotive is well dealt with in E. L. Ahrons, *The British Steam Railway Locomotive, 1825–1925* (1927) with a supplementary volume containing the story to 1965 by O. S. Nock (1966). For carriages see C. H. Ellis, *Railway Carriages in the British Isles* (1965). The train service provided by the later Victorian railways is analysed in H. S. Foxwell and E. Farrer, *Express Trains English and Foreign* (1889).

The history of railways in war-time is dealt with by E. S. Pratt, *British Railways and the Great War* (2 vols., 1921), C. I. Savage, *Inland Transport* (History of the Second World War, 1957), and R. Bell, *History of the British Railways during the War, 1939–45* (1946).

The history of most of the individual companies has been chronicled. Among the most substantial accounts are W. W. Tomlinson, *The North Eastern Railway* (1915), E. T. MacDermot, *History of the Great Western Railway* (2nd ed., 2 vols., 1964, with supplementary volume by O. S. Nock, 1967), and G. Dow, *Great Central* (3 vols., 1959–65).

Railways in London are part of the subject of the large and excellent *History of London Transport* by T. C. Barker and R. M. Robbins (2 vols., 1963–74). Other local studies are to be found in *A Regional History of the Railways of Great Britain* (7 vols. so far published, 1960–74).

Vol. IV of that work, *The North-East* (1965) by K. Hoole, contains an account of the Stockton & Darlington Railway, to be supplemented by Tomlinson's *North Eastern Railway* (already cited) and J. S. Jeans, *Jubilee Memorial of the Railway System* (1875).

The recent history of British Rail is dealt with in the Annual Reports of the British Transport Commission and the Railways Board, in the two "Beeching reports" (pp 136–7), in G. F. Allen, *British Railways Today and Tomorrow* (3rd ed., 1962) and *British Rail after Beeching* (1966), and in D. H. Aldcroft, *British Railways in Transition* (1968).

INDEX